THE AGONY THAT REMAINS

Photo by Jared Herrera

About the Author

Brandon Callahan grew up with an insatiable desire to learn everything he could about anything mysterious. He has been actively investigating paranormal activity in the field for many years and has developed a method of tracking potential "hot spot" locations throughout the world.

To Write the Author

If you wish to contact the author or would like more information about this book, please write to the author in care of Llewellyn Worldwide, and we will forward your request. Both the author and publisher appreciate hearing from you and learning of your enjoyment of this book and how it has helped you. Llewellyn Worldwide cannot guarantee that every letter written to the author can be answered, but all will be forwarded. Please write to:

Brandon Callahan
℅ Llewellyn Worldwide
2143 Wooddale Drive
Woodbury, MN 55125-2989

Please enclose a self-addressed stamped envelope for reply, or $1.00 to cover costs. If outside the USA, enclose an international postal reply coupon.

BRANDON CALLAHAN

A PARANORMAL INVESTIGATION
IN AMERICA'S HEARTLAND

Llewellyn Worldwide
Woodbury, Minnesota

The Agony That Remains: A Paranormal Investigation in America's Heartland © 2016 by Brandon Callahan. All rights reserved. No part of this book may be used or reproduced in any manner whatsoever, including Internet usage, without written permission from Llewellyn Publications, except in the case of brief quotations embodied in critical articles and reviews.

First Edition
First Printing, 2016

Book design by Bob Gaul
Cover image by iStockphoto.com/55746420/©shaunl
Cover design by Ellen Lawson
Editing by Aaron Lawrence

Llewellyn Publications is a registered trademark of Llewellyn Worldwide Ltd.

Library of Congress Cataloging-in-Publication Data (Pending)
ISBN: 978-0-7387-4793-4

Llewellyn Worldwide Ltd. does not participate in, endorse, or have any authority or responsibility concerning private business transactions between our authors and the public.

All mail addressed to the author is forwarded, but the publisher cannot, unless specifically instructed by the author, give out an address or phone number.

Any Internet references contained in this work are current at publication time, but the publisher cannot guarantee that a specific location will continue to be maintained. Please refer to the publisher's website for links to authors' websites and other sources.

Llewellyn Publications
A Division of Llewellyn Worldwide Ltd.
2143 Wooddale Drive
Woodbury, MN 55125-2989
www.llewellyn.com

Printed in the United States of America

Contents

Dedication   xi

Introduction   1

One: Dreams and Consequences   7

Two: Road Trip Begins on Route 66   15

Three: Welcome to Oklahoma   23

Four: Walk Part One   29

Five: Walk Part Two   43

Six: Investigation One   53

Seven: Follow-up and Homecoming 75

Eight: American Holocaust 79

Nine: Jason's Walk Begins 91

Ten: Jason's Walk Concludes 103

Eleven: Gerald the Storyteller 119

Twelve: Home Sweet Home 127

Thirteen: Team, Tahlequah; Tahlequah, Team 135

Fourteen: Side Effects 149

Fifteen: Flying Solo 155

Sixteen: A Dark and Stormy Night 169

Seventeen: The Geographical Connection 177

Eighteen: The Road to Affliction 183

Nineteen: The Event 205

Twenty: Back Home 235

Twenty-One: Marvin's Story 239

Twenty-Two: Jan and Brandon 249

Twenty-Three: Life Happens 261

Twenty-Four: Picking up the Pieces 267

Twenty-Five: One More Step 273

Twenty-Six: Back on the Road 283

Twenty-Seven: Looking for Answers 295

Conclusion *319*

Dedication

THIS BOOK IS DEDICATED to those who have suffered throughout the history of the world because of differences in skin color, religious beliefs, or culture. Remembering the atrocities of the past may help us avoid such devastations in the future. Our differences should bring us together and inspire us to open our minds and hearts. We should learn from one another and love each other as human beings. We should not stand in judgment of others, but allow ourselves to be open to the knowledge that what makes our kind great is our incredible diversity and the very differences that have historically torn us apart.

To those I have loved and lost and those that still remain. My endlessly supportive family and friends—you are my heart and soul. My wife, Nicole, and our amazing children, Zachary, Bailey, Evan, Charlotte, and now our sweet Agnes; you are my everything.

I remember those lost through great tragedy and only wish to do my part in remembering their sacrifices. People who suffered for no good reason other than fear and greed. The Native American community is still strong and proud. I consider myself blessed beyond words to have been accepted as family by Marvin and Gerald Allen, and Annette Stinnette. You have become a second family to me and I am forever grateful for your invitation into your lives and history. I am a better person for knowing you and the incredible story your lives provide. Your strength and courage amazes me.

To so many people who worked long and voluntary hours away from your family and friends, I thank you for your dedication and incredibly hard work. You are all like family to me. I am proud to call myself your friend and brother. There are too many to name for fear of missing someone, but you all are the reason stories will live on forever.

I must thank my parents, Jim and Bridget Callahan. I cannot imagine my life without the loving support you have provided all of us, and you have always put your family ahead of yourselves no matter what. My team, Courtney and Jennifer Callahan, Colleen McClernon, Jared Herrera, and Jason Buis: I could not do any of this without you. A special thank you to Jeremiah Norwood; you and I set out on an adventure that changed my life. It was a once-in-a-lifetime experience and I thank you for being by my side.

I also want to remember my inspiring Aunt Janice Callahan, my grandparents, Ken and Barbara Mitchell, and the rest of the Mitchell clan. You all have been ever loving and supportive throughout my life. I am eternally grateful.

Introduction

THE IDEA OF ROAD Trip Paranormal began with a simple conversation between a friend and me as we established the need for people to really dig deep into the culture of different locations throughout not just the country, but the world—from small-town America to the large cities that have established themselves as world superpowers of corporations with billions of dollars around every corner. Every city, state, or country has its own culture that has been developed over hundreds and thousands of years. The goal for Road Trip Paranormal would be to venture out into all different types of places and document the general thought process about the paranormal and the people's beliefs and outlook on unexplainable things. I have seen that the speed of life in larger communities in general removes a lot of thought from things that are not right in front of someone. Life moves fast and it seems more common now with the evolution of technology that many people are all too often so absorbed with the everyday details of life that they do not dig any deeper than what is on the surface of life. The goal of Road Trip Paranormal would be to reestablish that connection between culture and history and how we got to where we are.

I had determined the path of the first road trip would take me from Kansas City to New Orleans, and we would stop at many locations along the way to conduct investigations. I wanted to speak to the locals about the folklore that had been handed down from generation to generation and document everything I could. I had been working for months on developing a method that would lead me down the right path to find locations that had never been investigated, and I was hopeful it would lead me to many stories that may not have been told to the world. I wanted to open a window of opportunity to put these stories out in the world and allow people to reconnect with the history of this country.

I had been reading everything I could find that had anything to do with the study of ley lines throughout the world. Ley lines are said to be an alignment of significant structures and locations that have historical significance, usually marked with the location of ancient monuments, megaliths, churches, burial grounds, etc. The development of ley line research stems from different cultures from thousands of years ago that typically held the belief that there are certain locations throughout the world that hold a stronger natural energy level than most other places.

There happened to be a couple intersecting points in close proximity to my location in Kansas City, so I was able to head out and conduct some research and begin to test my theory in and around these places of intersection.

Two locations where I conducted research seemed to turn up interesting information that led me to wonder whether or not these intersecting points may draw in certain types of events. As I focused on historical research in and around the areas of interest where the lines seemed to intersect, I was able to find a lot of interesting occurrences that took place over many years. Most of the things I was able to find in and around these locations seemed to be of some historical significance. There seemed to be an abundance of burial grounds, significant religious locations, battlefields, and all sorts of different things that really made me wonder if there truly is a specific type of energy that may attract groups of people or events to these lines.

One point of intersection in the Kansas City area actually turned out to be in close proximity to the Kansas and Missouri state line. It isn't too far from a location that is widely believed to be one of the seven gateways to hell that exist on the earth. Stull, Kansas, has a dark history of stories that have been told for a very long time, leading many researchers to believe there is a cemetery in this small community with an extremely dark past and stories so outrageous that one of them includes the actual appearance of Satan on an annual basis. For years, Stull has been a destination for many people who travel from surrounding areas and places all over the world just to be disappointed to find that this small community does not easily open up about the folklore that surrounds it. There really is no documented proof that many of the stories are true. There is a cemetery in Stull and it has proven to be quite active, but the church that is the focal point of much of the lore has been torn down, and there is hardly anything left to prove it ever actually existed. At this point in time, if you are found uninvited at the cemetery, you will be promptly approached and asked to leave.

The locations surrounding the intersection of these ley lines near the border of Missouri and Kansas do have a lot of history. There are stories of Indian burial grounds that have in many ways been forgotten about over the years. I decided I would focus more on the ley line intersections so I could have a point on a map that I could approach and hopefully anticipate activity without throwing darts at a map and hoping to hit an unmarked bull's-eye. I felt like this was a really good start. Road Trip Paranormal would be born, but I needed to figure out the details of this maiden voyage, and I still needed a willing participant to accompany me on this trip.

At the time, I had been laid off from my job, so my schedule was not a normal Monday-through-Friday schedule. I was not going to allow this opportunity to slip through my fingers; I would put this trip together and I believed wholeheartedly that it would be the beginning of something amazing.

After several days of contacting people for this trip, I received a reply from my very good friend, Jeremiah Norwood. We put all the dates and details together and decided this was a perfect way to establish the Road Trip Paranormal name. We would head south and document as much as we could along the way, hopeful that we would be able to tell a memorable story to get this new idea off the ground.

The northeastern corner of Oklahoma, right where Kansas, Missouri, Arkansas, and Oklahoma meet, is home to one of the largest clusters of intersecting ley lines in North America. Upon beginning my research, it did not take long for me to find several reasons that this was a place of enormous significance. At this particular location, there were four very distinct lines that intersected together right near the small Oklahoma town of Tahlequah, so this is where I focused.

Tahlequah is steeped in history; unfortunately, most of it is tragic in nature. The main story that came up quickly after beginning the search for history in the Tahlequah area was the fact that this is right where the notorious Trail of Tears ended. This was the forced removal of several Native American tribes from their lands in the southeast territory of the United States. After forcibly and brutally removing them, the US government would lay claim to the lands the Native people had inhabited for generations. The displaced Native Americans were marched toward what was then the Oklahoma Territory. Many thousands died under inhumane and impossible travel conditions along the way.

I wanted to reach out to the Cherokee community down in Tahlequah to see if anyone was willing to welcome Jeremiah and me with open arms. The only reason anybody would allow us in was because we were truly interested in the history and the story; I wanted to find out if there could be a correlation between certain occurrences in history and the ley lines.

ONE

Dreams and Consequences

THE SUN ROSE ABOVE my neighborhood. Drained of all energy, I dropped the bags of equipment in a corner of the room, pulled the curtains shut, and fell to my bed. I could feel something inside me, something more than what was there before. Lying in bed, I could almost hear it—it was like I had a second heartbeat. It is difficult to explain what happens to you when a place has worked its way into your mind, body, and soul. With each trip to Oklahoma, it was like I traded a piece of myself for something else.

Nightmares plagued my sleep, unlike any I had experienced before. In these dreams I was present, not necessarily in my earthly body, but as a witness to some of the most brutal scenes anyone could imagine. I was forced to watch the tragedy and pain of the past without feeling threatened on my own. It was as though my humanity was being tortured through the unspeakable pain and anguish of innocent people.

Dreaming, I feel the teeth of the wind bite through my entire body. The brutal cold strips me of breath. My lungs burn. I walk toward a faint light, the only sign of anything in the angry, bitterly cold night. With every cautious step there is the crunch of newly fallen snow beneath my feet. The thorns of honey locust trees surround me, seeming to protect against any and all intruders. Suddenly the silence is broken not only by the angry howl of the wind, but with what sounds like screams and cries echoing through the labyrinth of the forest. The pain burns as I move toward the glow of the light, but still, I have no choice—I must get closer.

I hover at a distance from the camp, still buried in the blackness of the woods. The screams and cries are now deafening and accompanied by maniacal laughter. I am frightened beyond words and have no sense of what is happening, yet the light—a bonfire—still draws me closer. Suddenly, I stumble and find myself face-first in the snow. I scramble to my feet and look down at what brought me to the ground: a severed head—the body a few feet away. The lifeless eyes stare back. Fear boils inside me. I feel sick to my stomach and I trip as I back away from the man and fall again to the ground, only to find yet another body. I clumsily work my way back to my feet as the screams and the laughter get louder. I'm standing in a killing field of mutilated bodies of Native American men, women, and children. Most of them look to be frozen to the bone. It becomes clear they have been there for some time.

I struggle to breathe at this point as I am still drawn toward the illumination of the camp. I hear the crack of a whip followed by the scream of a woman and uncontrollable cries of several people. There is laughter; someone mocks the people who shiver in fear and pain. A whip cracks time and time again, followed by more screaming and more laughing. I can't turn away. All I want to do at this point is run, but I'm frozen, forced to witness the murder and abuse.

A soldier shoves a naked man to the ground, takes a knife from a sheath, and grabs a fistful of his victim's black hair. The man contorts with his remaining strength, but, weakened, he is no match for the soldier. The soldier smiles at the people huddled together. He saws his blade across the forehead of the Native, whose screams rise above the camp and fill the air. The sound of sliced and tearing flesh being separated from the man's skull is like pulling the reluctant peel of an orange, and the man goes limp in the clutches of a madman due to the pain. The soldier pulls his trophy from the upper half of the Native's skull and holds it high.

The fear, the anger, and nausea roil inside of me, and I beg to be allowed to leave this dreadful place. With the brutal scalping of the man, I can feel a sharp pain in my head unlike anything I have ever felt before. I need to get out of this hell. I am now seemingly frozen in place and all I want to do is either run or die. I can't take the screams anymore. They set my soul on fire.

The soldier, still smiling blankly, wipes his blade on his pants, and then he makes eye contact with me and slowly approaches the woman and her children. They are distraught, fixated on the lifeless body of their father and husband—their caregiver, protector. He is gone and there is nothing they can do about it but brace for their own fates. The mother dives in front of her children, but the soldier, snarling, kicks the head of a young boy. The man then grabs the woman and throws her infant to the ground. I don't want to look. I don't want to listen. The soldier looks back up at me with the smile on his face as he removes his boot from the remains of the baby he has just stomped into the next life. I can no longer breathe; I can't move. Why am I being forced to watch such evil? Humanity is gone and fear doesn't begin to describe the feeling. At this point it's a simple helplessness with the weight of a mountain.

This is a death camp. I see dozens of groups of men, women, and children huddled together, most looking like living dead. Some of them are mostly if not entirely naked, and I can see their ribs protrude as if the skin is strangling the body. Most of these people are in obvious pain and covered in lesions and bumps from head to toe. Their eyes show tortured souls begging to be put out of their physical misery.

I walk unseen—except by that soldier—through this torture camp and watch one instance of human putridity after another. My senses soak in every detail of the grotesque nightmare that surrounds me. Blood stains the snowdrifts and the unforgiving wind screams through the camp and carries this madness for miles around. This land is being purged of all that was once beautiful and good by these marauders masquerading as "American" soldiers. They are committing unforgivable crimes against not only these people, but also this land.

    I snapped awake, covered in cold sweat in a dark room. The sun had set; I slept through an entire day. I was still void of any energy whatsoever. I eventually went down to my office and worked for a few hours uploading all the data I had collected during the investigation. While the world slept, I reviewed audio and video we collected during this trip, all the while completely incapable of convincing myself that everything felt right. Nothing was normal, inside or out; something was wrong within me and I found myself suddenly frightened of what might be ahead.

    As the evening wore on, I couldn't shake the idea that I was being watched. Something kept creeping up my spine, making the hairs all over my body stand on end. I couldn't recall ever feeling like this at home. Sure, there would be things like this on a pretty regular basis during an investigation, but at home, I had never really experienced anything to this extent. I went out to the deck to smoke a cigarette when I heard a very distinct growling sound coming from the shadows of my backyard. Just as in my dream, I couldn't help but investigate, so I walked down the stairs leading to the backyard. I kept my eyes trained to the corner of the yard where the sound had risen from, three times now. Something glimmered—two faintly glowing eyes from the darkest corner of the yard.

The thing growled a deep, guttural, and now familiar sound. Not quite spooked yet, I figured it was a stray dog, but the dogs next door didn't react to its presence as they normally would. Now is the time to make my way back up the stairs and into the house, I thought. I hurried back up the steps, trying to remain calm—but I was overtaken by panic. I all but fell over myself trying to get to the top of the stairs and inside as quickly as I could. I felt like something was sprinting right at me, right on my heels, as I slammed the back door behind me and leaned against it to catch my breath. I was sure I was about to be mauled by something, and it spooked me.

As I leaned against the back door, still trying to catch my breath—*BANG!*—something pounded against the door. My heart raced; I instantly tried to reason with myself—a tree branch had crashed down against the deck and the back door. Surely I was just wired from the week. But I looked out the window and saw nothing—not even a stray dog.

I attempted to shake off what just happened, and after a few minutes, I mustered the courage to go outside to see if the growling creature was still around. It was as quiet as could be, no sign at all of anything out of the ordinary, so I went back inside. I had that feeling again that something was not right with me physically, and this something was building. I knew in my heart that the many warnings I had been given and stories I had been told were morphing into something other than mere warnings and stories. The puzzle pieces were falling into place and despite the many experiences leading up to this point, I knew beyond a shadow of a doubt that I had seen nothing yet.

This nightmare came without warning and was followed by a personal experience at home that made me feel unsafe. At this point, I wondered if those around me were still safe. I now knew why I felt like I was constantly being watched—I was being constantly watched. Were these signs to flee from the case or an indication I was truly about to uncover some long-buried truths? Regardless, I knew I couldn't stop. I needed to reaffirm my standing with my own soul and confirm that I was truly protected while being surrounded by such incredibly dark and powerful energy.

It's been months, and I'm still coming to grips with the reality of the situation I've voluntarily walked into. The horror stories I've been told about the past and present seem to be crushing me mentally and physically. This case has truly changed my view on the world. I've witnessed tragic and unspeakable things in my life, but this experience is beyond anything I've known. It's as though I'm being used as a medium or conductor to the past of the land. And whatever the energy is, it doesn't stop with the specific locations I've visited in Oklahoma—it's everywhere, and it's worked its way into my soul as was promised from the very beginning.

With each trip to Oklahoma, it seems to take longer for the darkness and the energy to dissipate, but I'm hooked on this story, this history—all of it. I asked for so much when I chose to dig as deeply as I could, and I've been shown exactly what I was asking for—the only question is whether I can handle it. Still, I have to keep working and I have to keep researching. Oklahoma is now part of me, a part that will be with me for eternity. The history blows in the wind and you can taste it and feel it with every breath taken. I connected with these people. They're some kind of second family now.

For a very long time now, I've believed that most cases worth working actually have a way of finding the investigator. I know there's a very specific reason I found this second family of mine. They gave me the opportunity to conduct as much research as I needed to and they were by my side the entire time, simply hoping to understand it better. This case had certainly found me; there was no doubt about that. Looking at this from a big-picture perspective, I can't be more thankful, all while being horrified in more ways than one. This was what being an investigator is all about: tackle and face your fears, learn as much as you can, and embrace the unknown if that's what you seek.

At this point, the darkness has set in, the storm is rolling through, and we are all in this to see what is out there. There is no turning back, no second-guessing. This adventure will be experienced from start to finish—assuming there ever is a finish.

TWO

Road Trip Begins on Route 66

JEREMIAH AND I ARRIVED in Galena and met up with my great friend, Russ Keeler, and his wife Julie. Russ had established his presence along the famous Route 66 in the Galena area and had access to a lot of places in this old town. Galena is known to be a very active town and from my previous experiences down here investigating with Russ, I was able to confirm there was an awful lot to be studied from these locations. Tonight's investigation would be focused on two different buildings, mainly an old bordello that Russ was working diligently with the town to restore, as it had fallen to ruins over the years of neglect.

We all got together and did a walk-through of both locations while Russ and Julie were there. Russ shared some information with Jeremiah as I wandered for a little bit before we set up all our equipment and began the investigation.

As the night went on, Jeremiah and I didn't experience a lot of activity in the first location. There were some unexplainable sounds—knocking and things like that—however, nothing really stood out. We decided after a couple hours to go ahead and set up two cameras and allow them to sit and record anything that might happen while we headed down to the bordello house. You would think this house was plucked right from a book of stereotypical haunted houses. The two-story Southern home was in tatters on the outside and the inside wasn't any better. A couple large, ominous trees stood out in the yard as though they were the protectors of the house. As we entered the house, there was an odd feeling to the environment. I had heard many stories about activity being off the charts in this house, but the few times I had investigated it, I had not experienced much, so I really could not corroborate a lot of the stories I had been told. I was hopeful we would be able to stir something up.

> Recently I had acquired some new equipment I was excited to incorporate into our investigations. I had become a very big fan of the Ghost Box *[GB]* as a resource that I believed was able to provide us with direction. I try to be careful to not consider much of what we receive from the Ghost Box as "evidence." However, attempting to explain some of the things

we got from it was next to impossible. So I gladly looked at it as a useful device that could simply assist in leading us down a path to eventually help provide some of the proof we were looking for.

The Ghost Box is a device that cycles quickly through AM or FM frequencies, providing a great source of white noise. In theory, the white noise allows spirits to communicate with us as we ask questions by speaking through the white noise that is provided. Because the frequencies pass at such a high rate of speed, it begs the question "how am I hearing a word or sometimes a series of words come from this box if the frequencies are changing so quickly?" Most times, when you are hearing a word or sometimes a series of words, you will hear them come from the box and they will be spoken by the exact same voice throughout the entire series. When this happens, you want to keep an open mind and understand there could be a natural explanation. However, I always suggest you do not dismiss something that is obvious even if you can't explain it logically.

I had recently upgraded my Ghost Box to a device called the P-SB7, also known as a Spirit Box *[SB]*. The P-SB7 swept the frequencies at a much higher rate of speed than the Ghost Box did, so in theory, you should receive even clearer messages. The Ghost Box did not sweep the frequencies extremely fast, so there were times that it was questionable what exactly you were hearing when the messages seemed to come through. With this new device, the sweep is at such a rate of speed that there is no confusion when you are hearing voices and words coming from the device. There is simply no way to explain away a clear sentence that comes through a device while the frequencies are moving at such a high rate of speed. I had quickly grown much attached to this new piece of equipment and could not wait to implement it on our trip.

The other fairly new piece of equipment I was happy to use on this trip is the RT-EVP recorder (real-time electronic voice phenomena). I had used it on other investigations, but had not had the chance to put it to great use as of yet. For the limited time I had used it, I was amazed at what it brings to the table. It had quickly become my favorite piece of equipment. As the recorder is doing what it does, it plays back on a delay through earphones I wear. I can adjust the delay and typically used it on a two to three second delay. The microphone that is built into the recorder is designed to pick up sounds on a lower frequency than what we can hear with our own ears. In essence, this recorder is like listening back to what has been recorded, and in theory, you can hear potential EVPs that are captured in real time. (Electronic voice phenomena *[EVP]* are alleged spirit voices unable to be heard with the human ear at the time they occur.) Best case scenario, this recording device would allow for real-time communication with the spirits as they verbalize whatever message they have. I had played back audio from my recorders shortly after conducting EVP sessions on investigations in the past, but I had a hard time imagining anything better than doing that as the question and answer session was going on in real time. I had been amazed at some of the things I was able to pick up as they happened with just a couple seconds delay. These new pieces of equipment left me very confident that I would be able to incorporate them into our investigation process, and I had high hopes of great progress and results.

As Jeremiah and I settled into the bordello, we decided to split up to minimize the cross-interrogation that sometimes happens during an investigation, so he would start on the first floor of the house and I would make my way up to the third floor attic space. Jeremiah reported little to no activity downstairs after almost an hour. I had a similar feeling in the attic, although I felt like there were eyes on me. We all know that inexplicable feeling of something or someone staring a hole right through your body and it feels like it is in your soul. As I was upstairs in the attic, I didn't feel like I was constantly being watched, but it came and went.

Two

I asked Jeremiah to come upstairs since the night to this point was very uneventful.

"Whoa, did you just—" Jeremiah stopped in his tracks and looked toward the pitch-black corner of the attic.

"Damn, you saw it too?" We had both just seen a very obvious, intensely black shadow peek out of the blackness just long enough for both of us to see it very clearly.

After a few very short seconds, it had disappeared back into what seemed like the darkest corner of the attic. We were unable to make our way to the corner of the attic because there was no footing at all. There were holes in the floor that allowed us to look directly down to the floor below, so we knew it was not safe to navigate with all our weight.

"So, you just showed yourself to both of us, right?" I began an inquisition and hoped to get some type of response.

"Can you make some type of noise just to confirm for us that you are up here with us?" I continued.

Before I could even finish my sentence, we both felt a cold blast zip right between us, as though a large gust of wind came out of nowhere and went right through us and headed downstairs. Jeremiah quickly went down the stairs and I followed him as quickly as I could. We both felt in our guts that whatever we had just seen might have just made a break for it, and it possibly may have wanted us to know it was there. Finally it seemed the night was coming alive after its extended slumber.

We made our way to the second floor where Russ had told us a ton of activity had occurred over the years he had investigated. I had no idea what we might have just encountered, so we split up again into different rooms on the second floor and continued our communication session.

I made my way into a room where Russ had reported being physically attacked one night, so I was curious if whatever we may have run into upstairs might be the thing that went after Russ. At first everything seemed quiet, so I decided to go ahead and turn on the Spirit Box to see if anything would be willing to reveal itself.

"This should make it easier for you to speak to me. Do you know who we are?" I began my questioning as the frequencies zoomed by.

"Russ said something attacked him in this room. Are you here?"

Nothing.

"We saw you upstairs; are you here?"

Nothing.

"I keep feeling cold air circling around me. Come here for a second," Jeremiah said from across the hall, so I made my way to him.

After a couple minutes, Jeremiah informed me that he no longer felt the cold air. I hadn't felt anything at all since I came in either. Frustration set in because I knew something was very likely here, but there was no communication at all.

"I was told that this house is unbelievably active, but you haven't shown us anything at all. I don't like playing games. If you have something to say, then get your ass out here and say it." I allowed some of my frustration to come out. I typically keep taunting to a minimum, but I let my frustrations get the best of me on that particular night.

My comment was immediately followed by a very distinct growling sound coming from the Spirit Box. Both Jeremiah and I looked at each other and exchanged a quick nod to acknowledge we both heard the same thing.

"Oh, are you pissed off? Who are you?" I tried to continue the communication.

"Over here." [SB]

A cold chill ran up my spine as though the message from the Spirit Box in my hand had come from the other side of the room.

We kept at it for a few more hours with no success until the sun began to peek over the horizon. We decided to pack up and call night one a success, despite being a fairly slow night. It was a simple reminder that we never know when and where anything will happen.

Jeremiah and I decided to cover some miles before getting some sleep, so we drove for about an hour to put us close to our second night's location in the northeast corner of Oklahoma. The next morning we packed up and headed to the next stop: Tahlequah, Oklahoma.

We met Annette in Tahlequah and followed her to our next location.

THREE

Welcome to Oklahoma

IT WAS A GLOOMY February day when I met the Allen brothers. There was a chill in the air, although it didn't cut the skin like the weather I left behind in Kansas City. The clouds covered the region like a blanket; the beauty of the land could not be disguised by an otherwise miserable day. Jeremiah and I were tired from the previous evening's events, but we were very excited to see what was truly behind the stories we had been told by Annette.

We met her and Marvin Allen waiting for us in the parking lot. Both of them seemed very happy to see us. Marvin was a very soft-spoken but large man; I saw him likely to be a very intimidating person to a stranger. Annette's smile was so warm and welcoming; she immediately came across as one of the kindest people anybody could ever meet. Marvin seemed extremely happy to have someone come down not only to conduct an investigation, but to listen to the countless stories he and his brother had stored in their minds for so many years.

We caravanned behind Marvin's truck as we drove out to what seemed like the middle of nowhere. We were quickly out of town and found ourselves on the notoriously winding roads of the Ozarks as we made our way toward the Allens' property.

Each mile felt like three as we traveled along the meandering roads. Taking in the surrounding beauty was nearly impossible with the driver's full attention needed to simply stay on the road. We were surrounded by incredible hills, deep woods, and openings to fields that might remind someone of a green hillside in Ireland. I had spent a lot of time in the Ozarks growing up, but I had never been to this part, known as the foothills of the Ozarks, and they were spectacular.

It was impossible not to notice how many broken-down or abandoned homes there were along the roadway. In this area, neighbors are typically miles away, not right next door. I quickly lost count of how many old houses I had seen with caved-in roofs or the bones of what used to be a structure. Every few seconds that passed, and every curve we left in the rearview mirror, I felt more and more isolated and it began to wear on my nerves a little bit. This would not be the first time I had investigated a location that would be considered in the middle of nowhere—that part didn't bother me at all. I really had a hard time putting my finger on it, but something was different about this drive. We were heading into the belly of the beast, and my stomach churned with the anxiety I typically feel when going into an investigation.

I noticed as we drove that the only thing rivaling the abandoned and broken-down houses along the road was the number of cemeteries. It seemed they were around every corner. Every culture has their own beliefs and approaches to how and where they bury their dead. My mind went back to the ley line map that had led us here in the first place, and I remembered that it is very common to see churches and cemeteries along these lines. The fact was that we were in the heart of an area that had several lines intersecting, and I began to take mental notes of all the signs I was seeing.

After what seemed like forever, Marvin signaled and we turned off the highway and headed for the back roads and farther into the unknown. As I turned, the only thing around was another cemetery and a small church. There was a strange feeling to everything at that time; my senses were on overload at that point. Most of the houses were seemingly livable but somewhat worn down. It was very clear this area was not heavily populated and everything seemed to be hand-built and maintained.

We came to what looked like a dead end as the pavement halted. We continued on the gravel road as we slowly made our way around a few more curves. There were no other signs of civilization, and it was clear we were heading to a secluded location. We were miles from anywhere; I loved it and hated it at the same time. These people seemed trustworthy, but there was a natural wonder as to whether or not we were making a good decision blindly following anyone to such a remote place.

Before long, Marvin slowly turned into the entrance of a driveway that led up a hill. Jeremiah and I followed him as we pulled up into a very large, gravel-covered circle drive. We came to a stop. I immediately noticed a small, run-down old house about thirty yards from the driveway, and I knew that would be one of our focal points of investigation. It had clearly been abandoned for some time. I noticed in the distance, at the other end of the circle drive, a house that seemed to be much more functional than the ruins to my right.

I took a step from my car and immediately felt as though I stepped not outside, but into a tomb. I had an overwhelming feeling of claustrophobia, as though I was being buried alive, but I was standing in a driveway during broad daylight. I hadn't felt that overwhelmed in a very long time. Something about my surroundings felt overbearing, as though I was being wrapped in a full blanket of energy. The energy was not subtle, it was obvious. It was so substantial that I felt panicked for a brief period before forcing myself to set the initial feeling aside and move forward with what we were there to do. I did not want that feeling to be obvious or even noticeable to anyone, including Jeremiah. I had no idea what to expect from what lay ahead, but I did know that I had an immediate feeling that something was going to happen; it felt as though it would be something very significant. I was engulfed by the unspeakable natural beauty and the elegance of this open land, yet my mind and body felt dread—I couldn't explain it.

The land demanded respect. Or maybe the land commanded respect, but my natural reaction to the feel of the air knew that respect was an absolute requirement. It was clear, day or night, that if you were lacking a certain reverence for this place, the ground might open up and swallow you whole. I knew within minutes of arriving that countless things were likely lurking about—things that could do with me as they pleased without limit or conscience. It was one of the most terrifying thoughts I had ever had. My mind was simply incapable of understanding the feelings that drowned me where I stood.

As I was wrapped in a warm embrace with Annette and a heartfelt handshake with Marvin, I noticed a man slowly walking down the circle driveway in our direction. He carried a walking stick that was nearly as tall as he was, and he yelled out, "Well hello there! Thank you so much for coming to see us!"

Gerald Allen, a smaller and frailer man than his brother, approached us with a smile that would light up any room. He was a very flamboyant man, the complete antithesis of his seemingly surly brother, Marvin. He clearly did not get around that well, as he used his stick as a crutch, but that did not stop him from giving us one of the warmest welcomes we could have ever dreamt we'd receive. As Gerald took the last few steps in my direction, his glowing face suddenly turned much more serious as he simply told me while pointing at the run-down looking house I had noticed on our approach, "That's where the demons live."

I knew immediately we were in for a very interesting walk-through of this spacious property. Jeremiah and I would have our work cut out for us and I was very hopeful that these nice people would help us find what we were all looking for.

FOUR

Walk Part One

AFTER GERALD'S OMINOUS INTRODUCTION, I was hesitant, yet I couldn't have been more excited to hear more. I was looking forward to our walk-through with the Allen brothers and Annette. She was clearly a very close friend to Marvin and I could feel her heart of gold from a mile away. There are some people in this world that simply exude light and love from their bodies no matter how well you know them; she is one of those very special people. It did not take long at all to feel completely welcomed by all three of our new friends. I knew there would have to be some trust built up, as there always is when it comes to very personal experiences. There was another potential sticking point that I knew we needed to discuss sooner or later. It is not very typical of Native Americans to truly open up about much with "city folk" like me and Jeremiah. The subject of the paranormal is a sacred and mysterious thing in almost all Native American cultures; I knew it was very much the case with the Cherokee people. To an extent, I was surprised the Allens would even meet us, let alone welcome us to their property to investigate.

Jeremiah, Gerald, Marvin, and I gathered around to get a little background before we headed out on the land to hear all the things they were itching to tell us. Gerald explained to us in detail how his family was left about three hundred acres following a treaty made with the US government following the Trail of Tears and the Indian Removal Act of 1830. I had conducted some research on this before we set out on our trip, knowing we would be coming into the heart of the land that saw this travesty come to an end. The idea that acreage was the price the government felt would repay a debt it had accrued with Native people made me sick to my stomach.

Gerald continued explaining that over the years and generations, for one reason or another, the family had to sell off pieces of the land, and they now only owned about thirty acres. What a majestic place we had found ourselves in. The property was home to some very thick woods that surrounded the abandoned house and ran all along the circle drive, all the way down to Gerald's house. Some of the wooded area had been cleared around both houses to make for a functional yard. The abandoned house had a lot of overgrowth that had formed in every direction. There was also a worn-down trailer that sat dormant next to the abandoned house. The circular driveway went all the way around the main property. The south side gave way to the woods that seemed to be watching our every move from the moment we breached the property line. The north side was protected by a cliff that fell almost straight down about a hundred feet. The top of the cliff had a wall of trees that kept the outside world from looking in. As I looked at the entrance to the circle drive, I noticed a very large and open field that was fenced in across the dirt road. For some reason, the first thought I had was that I was looking at a battlefield. In the distance, I could see more tree line and it was thick, but there was a vast opening in the field that was surrounded by hills on every side. The only breaks in the field were a few clusters of trees that had grown over many, many years. I could see a herd of cows in the field across the way and could faintly hear them. There were occasional barks from dogs in the distance, but other than the occasional animal, there was not much to hear out this far.

Gerald began to go deeper into the details of the property. He explained how once upon a time that was the family house, pointing to the abandoned house. Everyone in the house had many experiences with unnatural things over the years. He explained they had not spoken of these things in public with any locals for fear of being called "crazy"—not uncommon in our line of work. Jeremiah and I did our best to assure them we were not there to judge but to help in any way we could.

Even as Gerald and Marvin continued to tell us about their family and the history of the property, I was unable to shake the feeling of the air being different here. This ominous feeling would not subside, but it was beautiful beyond description. There was a certain peaceful feeling that accompanied such a somber environment. I did not know if I should love this place or run for my life.

The Allen boys began walking us through the property, pelting us with one story after another. Before I knew it, I was being told they see deceased ancestors all over the property on a very regular basis. This was the report that least concerned me, as they were telling stories of medicine men and women practicing good and bad medicine all over the area.

Gerald explained to us that because of that type of behavior, it wasn't uncommon to encounter different kinds of spirit energy that may have been summoned many years ago but never sent back from where it had been conjured. Dark beings and unmarked graves throughout the property and stories of death, murder, and curses came at a blinding pace. The ease with which these stories were being delivered was disturbing because it became more and more obvious that these men had led lives very different from those I was familiar with. I also began to understand a little better that there were many reasons Native Americans tend to keep to themselves and not include outsiders in their circle of trust. I considered it a great honor that these men standing in front of me were so willing to lift the veil of secrecy to allow us to see what they had seen and experienced throughout their lives.

"You wouldn't believe the cruelty families would show each other. There were witches everywhere. Their form of entertainment was to ruin someone's life by cursing them, their family, or their land. People would go missing or die due to unforeseen circumstances resembling illnesses, or freak accidents would happen. In some cases, people would suddenly find themselves in a position of such depression they would end their own lives for no good reason," Gerald continued.

He told his stories so void of emotion it was eerie. At that point, it had become a normal part of their lives, so in essence, paranormal was normal for them. This was a thought I marveled at because most people have an experience in their life and it changes them. These men had grown up with one occurrence after another, to the point where it was simply a part of everyday life. I had not yet collected any data to corroborate what I was being told, but they had nothing to lose and I had everything to gain from simply listening and learning.

As the stories went on, there were key words like mass graves, unmarked graves, curses, murder, suicide, and so many more, it became dizzying. I wasn't sure what type of case we had stumbled onto, but I knew in my heart that we had encountered something most investigators spend most of their careers looking for. In my mind I knew I couldn't allow the stories to sell me on the location because at that point, they were simply stories. When you are being told stories on that level, you must accept the fact that there is a chance you may experience something significant. Both

Jeremiah and I were impressed with these men and could not put into words how we both felt something special about this place. Until you begin to experience something, no matter what feelings you may have, there is still a shade of doubt in your mind—a need to truly dig in.

Gerald had an infectious laugh; he made his way around the property slowly with us as we clung to every word of his incredible stories. He gave way to Marvin here and there; they would share each other's stories and even the stories of other family members. Marvin carried a bit of seriousness with him that at first made him come across as rather gruff. It did not take long for him to open up to us, though; he had a thirst for answers to questions that had obviously plagued him his entire life. Marvin seemed to be very even-keeled; he seemed like the type of person that was very vigilant and always paying attention. He did not speak unless he had something meaningful to say, and he was not the type of person that offered small talk unless he had been coerced. The Allen brothers made us feel welcome, and they certainly piqued our interest with the history they had given us.

They led the way to the abandoned shack as we cut through the overgrowth that seemed to be protecting the house from intruders. We approached a side entrance, where the portion of the roof that covered this entrance had obviously fallen victim to a good amount of flames. That side of the house was burnt to a crisp, so obviously that was the first question that came from us.

"When was the fire? Do you know what caused it?" I inquired in Gerald's direction.

"That was an accident; it happened not too long after the house was abandoned in the early part of 2004," Gerald explained.

"An accident?" Jeremiah asked.

Gerald laughed and explained to us that what had been an innocent bonfire simply got out of control and caught that side of the house on fire. I was not entirely sure how to take that explanation, but I knew we needed to take the boys at their word. I reminded myself that the Allens had no reason at all to lie to us—unless they just wanted to win some kind of award for owning one of the most active properties we had ever encountered.

The four of us entered the house through the side entrance, and with every creak beneath our feet we were reminded that this house had been abandoned for nearly a decade, and it showed. The wood floors were in total disrepair, so we had to watch every step we took. The house was cluttered with a lot of junk: old dressers and tables, all kinds of stuff that had gone rotten over the years of neglect. From the side entrance, we entered a narrow and short hallway that led into the main part of the house. To our left was a bedroom and to the right was the kitchen. We took a left to enter the bedroom; as we entered, we could feel ourselves begin to sink through the floor. Jeremiah and I both found our way to a sturdier floorboard that ran the length of the room, attempting to keep our balance while avoiding the remains of the ceiling that was now dripping down to eye level. This house was straight out of a horror movie. Everything smelled old and moldy; the floors seemed as though they had an appetite for anyone daring to muster the courage to test the remaining strength in each board.

"This room was mine at one point," said Gerald. "Our other brother also stayed in here for a period of time. I was always afraid of this room because it always made me feel sad, and I was always scared of what may be looking in from the window," he continued, as his voice seemed less than enthusiastic at that point.

Jeremiah and I stood cautiously as we looked out of the large window that peered into the backyard area. About twenty feet away, the woods that seemed to have eyes everywhere stared in at us.

After a few minutes, we moved back toward the hallway as Gerald and Marvin made their way into the kitchen. I walked carefully over the boards in the hallway and crossed into the kitchen where I finally felt at least a little sturdiness beneath my feet. I was beginning to feel as though my ears needed to pop. There was a pressure building as though I was on a plane, but for the life of me, I was unable to satisfy the need as the pressure just kept building. I had felt this before and, if history was any guide, it was not a good thing.

CRACK!

"Shit! What the—" Jeremiah snapped, trying diligently to remove his foot from the hole he had just punched in the hallway floor. He stood with one foot in the kitchen and the other beneath the house. He looked up at me with a very concerned look smeared all over his face. We grabbed each others arms and I helped pull him from the hole.

"Well, I guess we need to watch our step, huh?" I quipped. We all got a little chuckle as we let Jeremiah's heart rate come down before proceeding through the rest of the death trap.

We gathered in the kitchen and Gerald was eager to fill us in on the details there.

"It was Christmas Day in 2003 when the house was abandoned. We were gathered in here and had some drinks to celebrate the day. Out of nowhere, it was like a bomb went off right here," Gerald was standing in front of some remaining shelves where their kitchen table used to be.

"It was like an enormous glass bowl or jar had been filled with more glass, and it felt like and sounded like it was dropped with as much force as you can imagine and landed right here. The force almost knocked me off my feet. It was a large glass explosion with no sign of any glass anywhere," Gerald told us. Marvin stood intently listening to the details, obviously affected in some way by being here.

"After that, we left. We had had enough and knew this had to be some kind of sign that we needed to be somewhere else. There were innumerable things that happened over the years, but this felt dangerous. It felt like we were being warned, so we listened and began moving the necessities out of the house and decided to leave the house to be on its own." Gerald trailed off toward the end of the story as though his mind was wandering. There was a hint of sadness with the brothers. They had shared many good memories of the house as their home for many years as children, but there was a constant backdrop of fear that came along with every positive story.

"I've never heard anything like that before in my life. What's in there?" I asked Marvin in an attempt to bring them both back to the present. It seemed as though they both had gone somewhere else in their minds. I felt like they were reflecting on a past that was sometimes very horrific, so I tried to snap them out of it as we moved along into the second bedroom that was attached at the far side of the kitchen.

"This was my room," Marvin said with almost no emotion.

We walked in and I noticed another room through an open door that led to the back of the house. I approached the door and took a step into the next room, which used to be a bathroom. There was really nothing but danger to step on. There was no floor to walk on, only broken wood and piles of junk that nearly blocked the entire way to the back of the house. I noticed there was a mattress in that room that was obviously many years old and a dresser with a mirror on it. There was no other furniture to be found in there.

"This is where we see the faces of three witches that look in from outside. Those old bitches are mean!" Marvin said with conviction as Gerald laughed.

"I hate this room; it still gives me nightmares," Marvin said as he began to move across the room and back toward the kitchen. At that point, the pressure in my head was becoming excruciating. I had not felt that way often, only a handful of times from past investigations; there was always a feeling that we had encountered something negative when I looked back.

The Allen boys continued to tell us stories about the house. There seemed to be an absurd number of experiences over the years in that tiny little place. The strange thing to me was the vast difference from one experience to another. It wasn't like a typical story we were being told about something that happens regularly. There were dozens of things that seemed very different or unrelated, but they were all packed into this tuna can of a house, and it felt alive.

"This is where I used to be attacked at night time. A lot of people have seen faces in that mirror." Marvin pointed to the mirror sitting atop the dresser.

Gerald slowly made his way to the front door of the house through the living room. The floor had depressed a foot or so in the middle. It was obvious the floor was not nearly as sturdy as it had once been, so we all knew we needed to be careful as we passed through.

"A lot of times when we used to take pictures in this room, from when we were really little kids, there would be a black shadow that would show up next to us. I remember Daddy showing me a picture years ago of me crawling when I was a baby and it looked like something was crawling next to me," Marvin told us.

"He used to take a broom handle and beat on the attic because whatever was in here would move around up there and scratch around. It used to scare the hell out of us kids. We could hear it growling and Daddy would just curse at it and smash the broom handle against the closest part of the ceiling to where the sounds were coming from," Marvin said as Gerald chuckled and nodded in agreement. He stood in the doorway on the front porch.

Marvin decided he was finished with being in the house and clearly let us know he wasn't about to walk through the living room, so he exited back into the hallway while avoiding the newest hole in the floor. He left out the side entrance where we had come in.

"You see, this land is the scariest place I've ever been, but there is no way I could ever leave. This is our home. Even this house, it was a house of horrors for our family for years, but in the end, we are attached to it. Sometimes the house seems to fend us off, though," Gerald said.

"Oh, sh—" Jeremiah stumbled.

The floor suddenly collapsed about three feet beneath us as Jeremiah nearly stumbled all the way from the kitchen and onto me in the living room.

"Um, what the hell, Gerald. Was that some kind of sign?" I asked. I felt like I was going to have a heart attack. I was so stunned; I couldn't even react in a normal manner. I just stood there, still as a statue, and hoped that Jeremiah wasn't going to end up on top of me.

Gerald burst into laughter and looked at both of us. "I don't like being in this house. I don't believe it likes us being here either."

At that point, we decided it was probably a good time to retreat and catch our breath. I felt like Indiana Jones jumping and nearly diving my way across the living room and out the front door. Jeremiah followed me out as we looked back inside and saw a three-foot depression that now owned the entire living room. We stood on the concrete front porch and were thankful to be standing on something solid. The house provided one of the worst cases of the "funhouse effect" that either of us had ever experienced. When floors are uneven or soft due to mold or rot, it is a natural reaction to feel dizzy or like your equilibrium is thrown off since you are standing on a floor and anticipate it being sturdy. When it isn't, the funhouse effect takes hold of your mind and physical body, which can make you feel like something paranormal is going on around you. We had to note how that could be a problem inside the house, although we couldn't let that deter us from the investigation.

Before we continued with the rest of the walk-through of the property, I couldn't help but peek back at the house and wonder if we had just been given several signs that we should leave this house as it was. The house forced emotion to the surface; it made me question whether I was convincing myself of something potentially paranormal going on inside or if there was in fact some force that now claimed ownership of the abandoned structure that was letting us know we needed to stay away.

FIVE

Walk Part Two

AFTER A FEW MINUTES of recapping what had happened inside the house, we decided it best to continue with our tour of the property. Both Gerald and Marvin indicated there was a lot left to see. Jeremiah and I made sure we were documenting every single thing that happened from that point forward. We had decided to take a subtle approach with our equipment until they were a little more comfortable with us, but it was clear that it was the type of place where you could not let your guard down even for a second.

We took our time walking around the perimeter of the house once we came down off the porch. One thing I had noticed right when we began walking around the property was how much of the land felt very soft. There had not been much precipitation to speak of recently, but with certain steps we took, we could feel our shoes just sinking into the ground.

It was unnerving—I had never really felt anything like it before. I wouldn't have been surprised if at any moment the hill we stood on caved in on itself. We noticed a lot of junk had been strewn about the backyard area. Nothing sinister seemed to stand out, although there was an old, broken-down wooden structure that was mostly hidden by the thick woods. It had just been a place for storage by design. We were able to see a good distance through the woods because at that time of year the leaves had not yet covered the trees.

"There are eyes everywhere out here. You can't walk through these woods without feeling like something is constantly watching you or spying on you," Marvin said.

As we had made our way around the backside of the house, I had the thought run through my mind on more than one occasion that we were being watched. It was strange that Marvin had mentioned that right at that particular moment. He was right—there seemed to be eyes in all directions and it was quite unsettling at times.

We made our way from the back to the front of the house, which was very overgrown. We had a discussion about the trailer that sat buried by nature and the fact that their brother had lived in there for some time before he was committed to a mental institution, given the notion he had gone mad. Nobody had lived in the trailer for a long time; it just sat there staring through the woods as though it might have something to say. There were several large trees in the front yard. Gerald told us there had been stories told over the years by many family members about children having been buried in unmarked graves on the property. He believed there to be at least three children that had been buried. He was unsure about a precise location. This was yet another instance that stunned me and touched me to my core as it became clear that these people were truly left to fend for themselves in many ways over the generations. They took care of their own; they took care of their family business and kept everything private. It was truly eye-opening.

As the tour continued, so did the stories. There were three other houses on or near these grounds that once stood, all of which had extreme reports of paranormal activity. The only other standing structure on the land was Gerald's current house. It stands about one hundred yards down the large circle drive from the old house on a small hill. The location where the two older houses used to stand is close to his current home, but there is nothing but foundation left. There is an iron arch that stands at what would have been the door of one of the houses, and in close proximity to the location of the other house is his garden. He claimed to have found many old relics while digging in his garden. He would find fossils and old arrowheads, all sorts of things that gave him proof of Native activity in the area well before his family came there.

They explained how once upon a time there was a picture of one of the relatives that was taken near the iron arch; in the picture along with that relative was a deceased old woman—likely one of the ladies of the family that had passed on in previous years. They continued to speak with ease about deceased family members walking the grounds all day and night. It was clear—this land was unique to us and we grew an immediate respect for it and the people that inhabited it over many generations.

As we stood near the iron arch, right next to the foundation of the old structure, there was a large tree that covered a good portion of where we stood.

"That is where our uncle hung himself. He also went crazy while living here, and one day he just hung himself. The scary thing about it was the fact that nobody could remember any emotion from him in the days leading up to it. He just strung himself up one day and was found dangling from that branch right there," Gerald pointed to a large branch that stood out on this large and eerie-looking tree. He had just pointed out the hanging tree and told us the story of his uncle taking his own life without so much as stammering. It was just another thing on the endless list of morbid things that had taken place here. It is always a little disturbing to hear about people committing suicide, especially in a way like publicly hanging oneself for anyone to see. This seemed strange to me. At that point, Jeremiah and I had to come to peace with the fact that we couldn't allow ourselves to be overwhelmed; we needed to be ready for anything.

Gerald then pointed up into the woods where we could see the subtle remains of what used to be an old wagon trail.

"There is a field up there on the other side of that fence where our grandparents would tell us stories about lights that would chase them in the night. These glowing lights seemed determined to run people down, although there were never any reports of anyone actually being hurt by one of them, but they were very common," Gerald began yet another tale. "We used to play in these woods all the time. Sometimes, when I was walking through the woods, I would be hit by a small rock or something. I just assumed it was one of my brothers stalking me and throwing something at me, but nobody was ever there. I would also hear loud banging sounds like wood being smashed against wood. It was creepy because you always feel like you have eyes on you when you are out here, and when things start getting thrown at you, you pretty much shit your pants," he laughed.

After Gerald told us this, Jeremiah and I looked at each other with a like mind. I asked Gerald if he knew what he had just said perfectly describes what most would say is very typical Sasquatch activity. He looked at me surprised and said he had no idea. He did say there had been hundreds if not thousands of reported sightings of such a creature throughout the area over the years. He personally had never seen one, but said there were endless claims of these types of creatures being in the area.

Why the hell not add Sasquatch to the list? I asked myself in my head.

"There were also several times when I was out in the woods and a small object would fly over my head—maybe cleared my head by about ten feet. It made a sort of zipping sound that reminded me of the Fourth of July and the fireworks that spin really fast and then shoot off faster than you can blink. It would just briefly hover over my head and then ZOOM," Gerald made a hand gesture to imitate the small flying object darting off into the distance.

So within the span of about three minutes, we went from demons and ghosts to Sasquatch and UFOs. All I could do was chuckle. I asked myself what the hell we had gotten ourselves into. Whatever it was, I was beside myself with excitement about the idea of investigating such a place.

"That's not all," Gerald continued.

"Of course it isn't," I said, and we all started laughing.

"There have been many times over the years where it would be pitch-black out here in the yard and suddenly the whole place would be lit up as bright as day by some kind of light. The light would sometimes last for several minutes; other times it seemed like it lasted for hours. I have never been able to see the source of the light, but it is blinding," Gerald explained.

"So the entire yard area, the woods, everything would just be lit up by something large enough and you didn't see the source?" I asked Gerald. Gerald and Marvin simultaneously nodded in agreement.

Marvin and Gerald proceeded to tell us about the "little people." These little people are allegedly very common in these parts of the Ozarks. They are said to live underground in caves and caverns that run under the hills. These creatures are known to be very sinister in the Cherokee culture. They are sometimes thought of as little demons. They can cause accidents, attack people, and cause chaos if they put their minds to it. I was wondering if it was possible that these little people might also be tied to the stories of the flying objects we had just been told about. Were we dealing with some type of mystical and evil fairy? Were we dealing with aliens? At that point it was a free-for-all and we were just trying to prepare ourselves mentally for what might lie ahead.

As we began wrapping up the walk-through, there was the sudden sound of an owl hooting in one of the nearby trees. Gerald stopped and looked to us.

"The owl has a lot of meaning in the Cherokee culture, but it is very significant when it comes to the spirit world. When you hear an owl, specifically in the daytime, it normally means there is impending doom, even death. That just now was the first time I have heard any owl during the day for a very long time. They are not common around here, especially during the day," Gerald said.

The owl has always been my favorite animal. I have never been able to put my finger on exactly why I am so enamored with them, but their strength, stealth, wisdom, and cunning instincts have always fascinated me. Hearing Gerald's explanation of the owl in the Cherokee culture struck me, especially after hearing something supposedly very uncommon. We had no idea what to expect in the coming hours. I felt in my heart that we were truly where we needed to be, despite the fact that what Gerald had just told us about the owl was extremely disturbing. I felt at peace and was full of anticipation as the time to connect with the land was quickly approaching.

When Gerald left, heading to town, Marvin told us a story he indicated he didn't want to share in front of Gerald. I knew there hadn't been enough trust established between the brothers and us for them to tell us every single detail, but I figured if we ended up researching their place for an extended period, we would build it over time. The Allens did indicate they would be interested in having someone do extensive research there, and Jeremiah and I let them know we would definitely consider it.

Marvin began telling us a story about being assaulted as a young child—and many times throughout his life. He mentioned that in the days leading up to our arrival he had been awakened right at 3:33 a.m. and found three deep scratches on his arm and three more on his chest. Marvin showed me the scratches—deep enough to have bled. He said it was pretty common for him to wake up at 3:33 a.m. We were told his nightmares were getting worse recently and a lot of the activity had kicked up ever since he and Gerald agreed to meet us. He thought the two things might be linked. I let him know that we would do everything we could to make sure we didn't stir things up and chance escalating everything. Marvin said he didn't really care if it made things escalate—he wanted answers and he asked us to do what we could to find them.

His story struck me to my core. I knew early on that we had a lot in common, but I knew at some point I would have to tell Marvin about my past, just as he was telling me about his. At that point, I just wanted to make sure he knew that we were there to support him and his brother, not to judge them. Marvin told us these stories and there was a very clear look of nervousness and terror on his face.

I was hoping the night would be eventful enough to warrant more investigations. We were there to help them find some kind of answers, and we were there to conduct research in a place that could be a huge stepping-stone in our quest to find answers. If even a fraction of what we had been told had actually happened, then we were standing in the middle of one of the most outrageous places we'd ever stepped foot on.

Who knew how many bodies had met their end in so many ways? Lives had been taken, tortured, damaged for eternity while there were lives that simply came and went like anywhere else. There was a feel to the air here that reminded me that all too often the land could not let go of its past. It refused to allow anyone here to forget what happened, even before the United States was established. For hundreds, maybe thousands of years, culture ruled with an iron fist—culture that would not forgive any amount of disrespect to the existence of these hills, trees, and valleys. That property felt unlike any other. I could feel the place entering my soul, and I wondered if it would be my doom.

SIX

Investigation One

FOLLOWING THE EXTENSIVE VISIT with Gerald and Marvin, Jeremiah and I agreed that we had not expected the extent of everything we had been told. We discussed our game plan and our focus for the night. We had to document everything we could. Telling the story of the land would be as important as anything else. We were determined to take the challenge no matter the cost. While discussing all the details, we understood the unfathomable potential of this place.

After lunch in town, we headed back to the grounds. We pulled in just as Gerald and his cousin were on their way out. They were going out for a while to get a drink. They stopped and got out to talk. Gerald's cousin introduced himself; Steve was a little freaked out because he had gone up to Gerald's house and asked whose car was in the drive. Gerald had explained why we were there and that it was one of ours. Steve then told

Gerald, "Oh, that must have been who I saw walk inside the old house as I pulled up." Steve said, he had seen someone clear as day walk from the front porch into the house as he pulled in. He just assumed it was the owner of the vehicle. He found out that was impossible, and he was shaken.

Gerald, Steve, Jeremiah, and I stood around for a bit talking before they headed out. As our conversation continued, Jeremiah's face grew suddenly concerned—the likes of which I had never seen from him. He quickly walked between all of us, his eyes set on the land next to Gerald's house about one hundred yards away. He turned pale in the blink of an eye. He then turned around and looked at me and said, "I just saw a woman disappear behind that tree," and he pointed in the direction. We immediately headed toward that spot to look around. When we arrived at the location where he saw the lady, we walked over the bed of leaves, crunching with every step. Within a few feet, we met the edge of a cliff that fell straight down. The apparition he had seen had made no noise whatsoever and simply disappeared behind a tree that was much slimmer than any human could be, but it never came out the other side. Jeremiah described her as having long black hair and wearing a flowery blouse. He said the blouse looked orange. What stood out was the long black hair; he did not see any facial features. He said it was as though an actual person was there, not something transparent.

"Dude, I have never seen anything like that in my life!" Jeremiah told me as we looked around in a state of confusion.

The fact that something so outrageous had happened around four in the afternoon made us wonder what might happen later that evening.

Unfortunately, I didn't see what he saw. The event had happened in broad daylight, and his reaction was unforgettable. With strange activity beginning so quickly, we knew the project had begun, whether we were ready or not.

"You see, something has been expecting you," Gerald told us as we met back up with him and Steve before they set out for a while.

Before we knew it, the sun had set and we were finishing our equipment setup. The amount of information we had been given about the reported activity on the property had us feeling like we needed to be prepared for anything.

The feeling of peace and tranquility that had lingered throughout the day had quickly left with the fallen sun. We began the investigation in the old house. We were running a couple different cameras and as many recorders as we could get our hands on. We had taken an overall electromagnetic field (EMF) sweep of the entire property without the slightest fluctuation on several different meters. For our investigative purposes, the lack of EMF throughout the property was very beneficial. The previous night in Galena, Kansas, we could barely use our EMF detectors since they were going ballistic at every turn, making the data unreliable. In Oklahoma, it was exactly as we had hoped—completely flat. Any true EMF fluctuation could be notable, so we had many meters running at all times.

Before we cut our way through the overgrowth to enter the house, I stopped at my car and grabbed a few pieces of paper I had printed out before the trip. I had looked up as many key words and phrases that I could think of that were translated from English to traditional Cherokee. I wanted to see if asking questions or saying certain words in Cherokee would provoke a reaction of any kind. For the purposes of telling the story, all questions have been written in English. Something notable that came from this practice is that all responses I felt I received during the question and answer session incorporating Cherokee words and phrases seemed to come across on the audio as English. There were instances when I asked a question using Cherokee and received an intelligent response in English. This is unexplainable to me, but I found it very interesting.

As we entered the house, Jeremiah made his way to the room where the witches were reportedly seen peering in through the window and their faces in the mirror. He made himself comfortable as I stood in the kitchen area and ran the RT-EVP recorder. This was going to be a key device as theoretically it should allow me to hear responses in real time as we got them, due to the fact that it plays back all audio on a two-second delay.

Keeping in mind I was not able to hear all responses in real time, we gathered a lot of information in our review later on. Some of the data was so disturbing that I was content that I did not pick it all up real-time. For example, upon review, about one minute into my first recording, I had asked, "Are you in here?"

The response I received just three seconds later was simply: "Yes, we are."

Just about seven minutes into the recording session, I believed I heard my name. I asked Jeremiah if he had said my name, and he said nope. I knew what I heard though, and sure enough, I absolutely heard my name when listening to the playback. It was quick and gruff, but it was my name being spoken very clearly.

We could feel something all around us. It wasn't just in this house—we felt eyes on us all over the property. We could feel it coming from every direction and it did not feel welcoming at all. It felt as though it was waiting for us to make a mistake or waiting for an opportunity to manipulate our actions or thoughts in a way that would not be good or healthy.

My senses were on high alert after hearing my name. Just because things seem quiet on an investigation does not mean nothing is going on. Until something significant happens, there is always the thought that minds could be playing tricks. We had felt eyes watching us and my ears needed to pop, but hearing my name spoken by someone who was not visible let me know quickly that whatever we were dealing with was not only there, but extremely intelligent.

I proceeded with my line of questioning. Jeremiah sat quietly in the other room, soaking in anything odd that may have been happening.

"Get out!" [RT-EVP]

Before the line of questioning started, I heard a very scratchy, irritated voice in my ear.

"Why do we need to get out? We have been invited here; we are here to find answers. Can you please tell me who you are?" I attempted to roll with the command I had heard in hopes of conversing with this grumpy voice.

Jeremiah and I continued to lob questions, and tensions seemed to steadily increase throughout the entire house.

"Anything going on back there?" I asked Jeremiah. He confirmed nothing out of the ordinary other than mentioning that he felt a little nervous for some reason.

"Brandon, hey!" [RT-EVP]

"Did you just say my name, dude?" I asked Jeremiah.

"No, I didn't say anything," he replied.

I had been looking at Jeremiah from the kitchen with the living room to my right when a clear attempt at getting my attention came from the right side. I was getting a little flustered because that was the second time I had heard my name come through the headphones. I hadn't officially introduced myself by name—this was by design. That didn't seem to matter; whatever was there clearly had my name, whether I provided it or not. The second time it sounded like the same voice I had heard before, but it was much closer. It was as though something was right next to me and it was unnerving. I made sure my camera was pointing into the living room, where it seemed the voice had come from. I hoped to capture anything that might appear.

"I keep hearing shuffling or something in the living room," I told Jeremiah, peeking in to see if anything stood out.

"I am hearing something similar in the room across the way," he told me, referring to the inaccessible room attached to Marvin's old room.

"Something is freaking creepy here, dude. This is weird. I keep hearing my name and it's loud!" I told Jeremiah as he nodded in agreement to the fact that something felt very strange.

"Come here if you dare to." [RT-EVP]

Unexplained giggling. [RT-EVP]

I heard a very obvious giggling sound come from the living room in the same direction the shuffling had been before. I had to investigate further; I slowly began to make my way around my camera and the tripod. I was making my way into the living room to get a closer look.

As I took one final step toward the living room, suddenly a black figure that stood about three feet high glided across the living room. It went across the opened front door and toward me as though it was coming after me. I froze instantly, knowing my camera was behind me. The figure disappeared when it came within about five feet of me—my shocked momentum took me backward as I tried to freeze as best I could in an attempt to stand my ground.

"What the—; dude, come here, now!" I tried to get Jeremiah over to me as quickly as possible.

"What happened?" He asked as he approached me from behind, still frozen in the doorway between the kitchen and the living room.

I tried to explain to him as best I could about the figure I saw coming at me, and we quickly rewound the camera to see if we got a shot of it. Unfortunately, my hunch was true: I had placed myself right in front of the camera when everything went down, so we did not get a shot of the figure moving. We ran it back a little farther and were able to see what looked like a mist floating around near the front door, which was right around the time I heard the giggling and my name. Things had picked up very quickly, and it was clear that interacting with whatever was there was not going to be a problem.

We tried to find other explanations for what had just happened. I rewound and played back the audio recording of the giggling and my name being spoken. Jeremiah was floored. He confirmed how loud and clear everything was and he was stunned he couldn't hear it with his own ears as it happened.

"That is insane, dude. Unreal," Jeremiah said.

"The thing that gets me is the front door being wide open—we had it closed earlier and didn't open it yet. When I saw that thing, I couldn't see through it when it passed by the door. Right now we can see outside, the trees and everything with the faint light, but when it passed by the door, the lower part of the view was blocked by this thing. It looked solid," I said.

"No shit, you're right, we closed it when we left earlier. I know I didn't open it," Jeremiah confirmed. We both took a deep breath and tried to regain our composure. It doesn't matter who you are or how many investigations you have conducted in the past, when a series of events like that happens, your natural reaction isn't something that can be controlled or anticipated.

We settled down for a few minutes. I then had a chance to get pissed off with myself because I stepped right in front of the camera at the exact wrong moment. It was a bit of a letdown, but at that point, we were both convinced that it would likely not be the last chance to capture something on video. This tiny little house was hopping and it took almost no time to show its teeth.

We spent a few more minutes trying to come up with some type of logical explanation, but we really had none. Of course, there will always be a slight sense of wonder unless you are the one standing there watching this little black figure come at you, but we could not find anything that stood out as a possible explanation as to what had just happened.

"Hmmm." [RT-EVP]

"Seriously, what the hell! Did you just mumble or something?" I asked Jeremiah.

"No man, I didn't say anything," he told me with a chuckle.

We both knew that whatever was going on seemed to have its focus on driving me crazy. It was as though the more we tried to figure something out, the more distracted we were going to be. It was phenomenal; we just kept rolling with it as best we could.

"So you remember the stories they were telling us about the black mass that would show up in all the pictures, specifically when the pictures were taken in the living room?" Jeremiah reminded me.

"Hell yes dude, that is crazy! He said they were about three feet tall too. I swear whatever this thing was, it was about three feet tall and it was pitch-black. Crazy!" I thought out loud, ending with a chuckle—I was pretty stunned at that point. We had experienced something almost exactly as it had been explained to us by Gerald and Marvin.

It was an energizing feeling, knowing we were making progress. The Allen boys had given us an overwhelming number of stories, and to that point, they were making a lot of sense.

We ended up going back outside for a bit, leaving some recorders running in the house in hopes of catching anything that might be going on while we were not in there. It wasn't long until I noticed Jeremiah's attention had been turned toward the sky. He told me to look up.

Having spent five years in the Air Force, I like to believe I have a pretty good handle on what is and what is not a plane. Of course there were many Air Force bases in the surrounding area, and there was an outside chance the object could have been something military. We had no way of proving it though. The object in the sky was constantly illuminated, not blinking as most known flying objects would. It was very high up in the sky, much higher than any plane I knew of could have been flying. It was flying at a steady pace, but as we watched it, it seemed to slightly slow down before picking back up to its original pace, gliding across the nighttime sky. We attempted to film it, but it was just too high up to get a good shot. After about three minutes, it took what looked like a meandering and lazy left-hand turn and began to elevate until it disappeared. We watched and watched until it disappeared into space, never making any sounds.

"Dude, I have seen and read some crazy shit in my day, but I have never seen anything even remotely like that in the sky," I told Jeremiah, trying to wrap my brain around everything going on.

"That was insane. It was moving way too fast to be a satellite. That sucker covered some ground!" Jeremiah replied. We both stood with our eyes stuck on the beautiful, star-filled sky.

Both of us had just seen our first UFO in person. This was the true definition of a UFO, an unidentified flying object, and it was remarkable. Was this some kind of alien ship in the sky that we were watching? I had no idea, but the one thing I was sure of was the fact that it was something we could not explain.

After only several hours, there were already too many things that had happened that we could not explain. After experiencing these strange things, what had been described to us by the Allen brothers suddenly did not seem so farfetched. The night had only just begun, and already we had been stunned with all the strange occurrences.

Shortly after the UFO incident, Marvin got home from work and pulled up a chair to observe some of the things we were doing. Marvin seemed to be most affected in a negative way by the things that had happened over the years. Recently, everything happening also seemed to be aimed in his direction. It was apparent both he and his brother had been deeply affected, but for some reason, Marvin seemed both distraught and intrigued at the same time. He was also very welcoming to us, reiterating many times during the stories that he is not crazy. I believed we had given him a sense of confidence because we had explained to him several times that we were used to hearing extremely odd reports of activity. He quickly took an interest in what we were doing and asked if we could keep him updated as best we could as to what may have been going on. He was welcome to join us at any time if he felt comfortable doing so.

Marvin seemed happy that we had experienced several things because it confirmed in his mind that he was not crazy. It wasn't that he wanted us to experience traumatic things; it was simply that he wanted to know someone without bias could relate to him.

Static sounds came from Jeremiah's walkie-talkie, pause, more static sounds emanated from the walkie-talkie. "*Help me,*" the voice of a child came through.

"Dude! What the—" Jeremiah gasped as we looked up in astonishment at one another.

"That was a fucking kid, dude! It sounded like it said '*Help me!*'" I jumped in.

"Holy sheeeeit," Marvin seemed to be struggling to catch his breath.

Both of our walkie-talkies had been somehow manipulated at the exact same time. We heard the sound of static as though someone was calling in and then we heard the voice that haunted me from then on. I immediately got another recorder out and pressed record so I wouldn't miss anything in case it happened again. Sure enough, the voice came across the walkie-talkie and the words "help me" came through as clear as day.

We had been carrying walkie-talkies all night but hadn't even touched them. The walkies were only good for about a mile with a good line of sight. We were so far away from the highway, and really any other form of civilization, it was obvious that it would have been next to impossible for someone to be on the same frequency to communicate with us. A child's voice clearly saying "help me" seemed like the most absurd thing we could think of. I was unsure if we should try calling out on the walkie, but we decided to set them down with a recorder next to them to see if it happened again.

I took a deep breath and enjoyed a sigh of relief knowing I had my best recorder, the Zoom H2, running as the incident happened. One of the strangest things about what had happened was the fact that the words did not sound like a child in distress. The words were simply spoken and they came across as clearly as possible.

All three of us agreed that there was something in the air right then that seemed very strange. Marvin was enthralled with what had just happened. After a few more minutes, Annette pulled back up and joined us. She sat next to Marvin as Jeremiah and I decided to head back into the house.

As we entered the house, we sat on a couple of the tattered couches that had been left behind so long ago. We wanted to see if anything would happen in the late hours of the night that would even compare to everything we had experienced. Our energy was running on empty at that time, so we sat down waiting.

Static came from the walkie-talkies. Several times each walkie was activated and it seemed as though someone was on the other end, but there were no words.

"Dude!" I looked at Jeremiah, he looked back at me, and we both just waited. We refused to touch them, as we wanted to see what might happen without manipulating them in any way. Again, we heard the static as though someone was pushing the talk button from another radio.

Heavy breathing began coming through the walkie-talkie. Heavy breathing that sounded angry came through the radio over and over.

The breathing stunned us; we had heard the voice of a child before. This breathing seemed maniacal and extremely aggressive. Both of us were nearly frozen by what was going on around us. The air in the house was suddenly freezing. It had been chilly all night, but now it was frigid. We had not seen so much as the slightest fluctuation on any of our EMF equipment all night, and suddenly the K-II meter was going crazy.

"Dude, what the hell," I whispered to Jeremiah.

"Whatever that was sounded pissed off!" Jeremiah said.

Both walkie-talkies clicked on again with more heavy breathing. Accompanying the breathing was what sounded like laughter in the background. The breathing continued as though there was a mouth right on the speaking end of the radio.

"Oh my God, dude, did you hear that laughing! This is creepy!" I said as Jeremiah nodded.

"Yeah, I heard it; look at the K-II," he said as he steered me in the direction of the meter.

The K-II meter lights were on. Normally one might see a couple of the lights blink. Sometimes three or four of them would light up for a brief period of time, but now all five lights were on as solid as they could be. Every time the walkie-talkies chimed in, the lights on the K-II seemed to fluctuate with the sounds that were coming through. Radio frequencies can and do have an effect on the lights on this device, so we were not surprised at all to see them moving when the radios clicked on; however, the lights were not going off. Neither of us had ever seen the meter behave in that manner.

Both walkie-talkies activated again and the breathing continued into the microphone of the walkie. In the background, the voice of the child could be heard again as "Help!" struggled to come through over the powerful and seemingly angry breathing. Several words came through following the child's cry for help that sounded like a very angry voice. After review, "Look in back," is what had been recorded.

"No way! What the—I don't—" my words were now struggling to escape my mouth.

"What did it say?" Jeremiah asked.

"Can you talk to us through these walkie-talkies?" I asked the only question I could think of. I was just hoping my question would prompt a real-time response.

"*Yes, I can.*" Angry, yet mechanical-sounding words came clearly through the other end of the radio.

"NO WAY!!!" We both lost our composure at that point.

The same angry, mechanical voice had come through and answered a question just seconds after it was asked. Only Jeremiah and I were there to hear it. I had not touched the walkie-talkie. That was the design of how we conducted the experiment with the radios from the minute they began acting in such a manner. The call button was not pressed, the radio was not touched, I simply asked a question that only someone in the room could hear and it was answered clearly and immediately through the radio.

We had brought the radios with us for safety; we had no idea they would become one of the most valuable pieces of equipment we brought with us. Both of us asked a few more questions as we sat in awe of what had just happened, but we received no response. The K-II meter flattened out and was no longer responsive; the radios went silent. We were both still breathless.

The night had begun to wind down. The air seemed to lift and the activity in the house slowed to a crawl, as though all the energy had been spent. Both of us felt the effects as well; we were quickly running out of any remaining energy. Jeremiah, Marvin, Annette, and I decided to walk down the dirt road. There had been several witnesses over the years that had reported seeing a lady riding a horse at night. At that point we figured, "What the hell, why not." Marvin had made it very clear he did not feel comfortable walking on the road, but he agreed to accompany us. As we walked, we chatted about the night's occurrences.

As we got farther down the road, we all agreed that there was a pretty distinct feeling of being watched. The feeling was common when it came to being in a remote location in the dead of the night. It didn't necessarily indicate that something paranormal was going on; it was just a natural, uncomfortable feeling that was difficult to shake.

We passed slowly by another dirt road that turned to our left and seemed to go a long way back. The slow incline of the road eventually came to a peak before falling off beyond eyeshot. Marvin told us that down the dirt road were the remains of one of the notorious witches that had terrorized the community many years ago. That was Minnie Cotine's cabin. It burned to the ground while she was inside; she burned alive. Nobody ever figured out what caused the fire.

We approached a stopping point down the dirt road and decided it was a good time to turn around and head back. As we walked back, the large field we walked parallel to seemed like it came to life. The large group of cows seemed to be spooked, although they hadn't seemed to be bothered by our presence before.

"Did you just hear growling?" Marvin asked us.

Nobody else heard anything. We continued chatting about the history of the area and the community as we made our way back down the dirt road.

A loud roaring growl echoed through the air. [EVP]

The cows kicked up again in an inexplicable uproar, making the situation uncomfortable for everyone.

"Seriously, this is just crazy," Jeremiah said.

"I told you brother, you won't believe it, but it happens," Marvin said in an almost proud manner.

When we returned, Jeremiah reviewed his recording of the audio he collected during our walk.

"Dude! You have to hear this," Jeremiah said as he joined us.

Jeremiah pressed play on his recorder and a loud, echoing, roaring growl came from what seemed to be the small wooded area in the field where the cows roamed. Almost immediately after the sound, the cows were in an uproar. We did not hear the sound as it happened, which led us to believe it had been captured in the same manner as we capture EVPs, since we did not hear it with our own ears.

"Holy shit!" I said while laughing, "What the hell is that?"

"I know—it's insane. I didn't hear anything like that at all," Jeremiah confirmed.

"Was that what you heard growling, Marvin?" I asked him as he shook his head from side to side.

"I don't think so. It didn't seem loud enough to echo; it was like a grumbling sound from what I heard," Marvin replied.

As Jeremiah and I listened to the audio he had just captured, I decided to go back and listen to the audio from inside the house. I wanted to figure out what we had heard from the radio. We were unclear what the words were in one instance because they came out of nowhere to interrupt the angry breathing we had been listening to.

"Look in back."

"Damn," I said.

We were both forced to remember a lot of what we were told earlier in the day, referring to the energy and forces that clung to the back room in the house and the backyard area. We wondered if the voice had referenced the alleged unmarked graves.

When I reviewed the audio on my recorder that I was running during our walk, I picked up the exact same sound that Jeremiah did. It would be a very rare occurrence for an EVP to be captured on more than one recording device, even if they were in close proximity to one another.

When we discussed the roar that Jeremiah had captured on his recorder, I reminded him of the theory I had about Sasquatch. I had always wondered whether or not these creatures might exist, but could they also have the ability to communicate in a manner that we cannot always hear with our own ears? If they do exist, they must have a way of existing and communicating without being detected. I wondered if these creatures might be able to navigate between physical dimensions. It brought up many questions; however, what I heard on the recording sounded like the closest thing I could ever imagine one of these creatures sounding like. There was no way this noise came from a cat, bear, bird, or anything else I could think of. It was quite perplexing and it now raised questions I hadn't had reason to take very seriously throughout my career.

Due to exhaustion, we decided it was a good time to go ahead and pack up our equipment and head out. I talked with Marvin and Annette and confirmed I would be back as soon as I could to continue our work. We said goodbye to our new friends and headed to yet another less than desirable motel. We wanted to get a couple hours sleep before heading to our friend Russ's house the next day.

When we arrived at the motel just off the highway, we got into our room and Jeremiah decided he was going to take a shower. Once he went into the bathroom, I grabbed my recorder and went outside so I could log some notes from the evening. So much had happened that I couldn't settle down. I was outside for about five minutes before heading back into the room. I went to put my recorder back in my bag with the rest of my audio equipment and noticed my camera was lying on the floor a few feet away from my bag. I never left my equipment lying around, so this was very strange.

I was standing next to my bed and just scratching my head, wondering how in the hell my camera ended up outside my bag.

Jeremiah came out of the bathroom a few minutes later. "Were you in there this whole time? You didn't come out after you went in, right?"

"Nah, I could have slept in that damn shower. That was amazing," he told me.

"So you have no idea why my camera ended up over here?" I asked as I pointed to it a few feet away from my bag.

My mind went back to earlier in the day when both Gerald and Marvin had mentioned how careful we needed to be about things following us. The subject had come up more than once throughout the day and evening.

"No man, you didn't leave it there?" he asked me.

"Nope, I went outside for a few minutes to take some notes and came back in and it was right there," I explained.

"What the hell, dude?" he asked.

We both wondered what exactly we had stumbled across over the course of the day and night's events.

SEVEN

Follow-up and Homecoming

JEREMIAH AND I NEVER knew the meaning of exhaustion until we were on the final leg of our maiden road trip. We stopped at several places on our way to New Orleans and saw some really interesting things and places. We agreed that the trip had been very productive, but we were both ready to be home and back in our own beds. I had spoken to Marvin about stopping back through on our way back, so that was what we decided to do. We felt the need to swing back through Tahlequah as the final stop on our way home.

We had initially set out to conduct another investigation on the last night of our trip, but a scheduling conflict with Jeremiah's work forced him to get home pretty early in the evening. We ended up stopping in on Gerald early that afternoon, and he took us around town to a few places he wanted us to see. Everyone involved had agreed more in-depth research of the land was a necessity in an attempt to find answers. We felt a long-term project could provide an incredible story and educate many people. It felt like the type of place an investigator could spend an entire career searching for and never find.

Gerald took us to one of the family cemeteries and he pointed out a few notable graves and told us a few stories. There were an overwhelming number of concrete blocks that represented gravestones. It was a sad and sobering reminder of the humble environment we were standing in. Gerald also told us about the other family cemetery that was farther away from everything. It was hidden deep within the maze of dirt roads that wind all throughout the area. It was a place nobody would go, especially after dark, because it had been said that it was almost a certainty that something was going to follow you out of there if you intruded. The place sounded like it was straight out of a nightmare; we determined we would check it out at a later time.

By the time our tour ended, the sun was setting behind the hills. Jeremiah packed everything up and headed home and I stayed for a few minutes so I could talk to Gerald and Marvin. They wanted to hear more about the trip we had taken, so I filled them in on all the excitement we had encountered along the way. We also spoke a little more about the project we decided to pursue.

After we sat and chatted for a while longer, I decided it was time to go ahead and hit the road so I could get home and get rested up. There would be a lot of work ahead of us in the coming months, so I said my farewells to the Allen boys and headed back to Kansas City.

I arrived home in the middle of the night and could not get to bed fast enough. I had gone over to my girlfriend's house since I had not seen her in over a week; I thought I would surprise her and climb into bed. She woke up long enough to greet me and we lay as close to each other as we could. I couldn't recall a night in my life that I had ever felt so comfortable or happy. I fell asleep instantly.

I found out in the morning that she and her three-year-old daughter had been kept awake for a couple hours during the night by what she called obvious knocking. She said it always came in sets of three and seemed to come from the closet. The knocking stopped whenever she got up to try to find the source. I asked her why she didn't wake me up, but she said she didn't want to bother me because I was so tired. It seemed to be an odd occurrence that happened only after I arrived.

She and I jokingly decided that the souvenir I had brought home from my trip was "The Knocker." There didn't seem to be anything sinister about it, so we just left it as a joke and moved along. The next couple times I slept over there, "The Knocker" showed up again; I actually experienced it too. It was very strange and it seemed to last for a varying amount of time. She had mentioned it never happened when I wasn't there. I kept going back to the discussion I had with Gerald about the tendency for these things to follow people home. It was always in the back of my mind, but I had not experienced anything else out of the ordinary to that point. Whenever he seemed to show up, our little joke went on, always acknowledging "The Knocker" as we went about the rest of our night's sleep as best we could.

I got in touch with Jeremiah after we had been home a few days so I could thank him again for accompanying me on the trip. I let him know that I was planning on making it back down there as soon as possible. Jeremiah was not going to be as involved with the Oklahoma project as he would have liked, so I let him know I would get together with my crew and we would take the reins on the project. I told them all about the trip, and we all unanimously accepted the challenge that lay ahead of us.

EIGHT

American Holocaust

OPENING THE LINE OF communication and trust as an outsider to the Cherokee community was a difficult task. One of the country's ugly secrets for many years was the brutality and wickedness that came during the process of removing Native people from their homelands in the 1830s. I dug deep into the history of the Trail of Tears; it became clear to me that a lot of information had been disregarded and covered up throughout the teachings of American history. I collected as many anecdotes and stories as I could from the people I worked with and met down in Oklahoma. I felt it was very important to collect stories that had been handed down—stories that would not be found in any textbook.

Year after year, "Old Hickory"—Andrew Jackson—spoke about the necessity of removing the Native Americans from their homelands to further the American way of life and grow the economy, claiming it would do the same for Native Americans.

My research flowed into my dreams; it was as though I was transported back in time in order to see, hear, and feel the pain and anguish the Natives were put through by the government of my ancestors.

The following Andrew Jackson quotations are noted from timeline excerpts from annual speeches made to Congress:

> It will be my sincere and constant desire to observe toward the Indian tribes within our limits a just and liberal policy, and to give that humane and considerate attention to their rights and their wants which is consistent with the habits of our Government and the feelings of our people.
> —*Andrew Jackson, March 4, 1829*

Cries pierced the silence of the surrounding woods as the snow continued to fall. The men, women, and children barely had cloths to cover them as they huddled together in their makeshift imprisonment. The hunger and thirst they felt had taken a toll and had claimed the lives of many as they saw the devil lingering in all directions. The crack of gunshots rang out as a firing line dispatched another group because of their insistence for food and water and blankets to warm their children with. The devil had once again succeeded in quieting the unreasonable men; the pile of lifeless bodies grew and became a windbreak for those that remained. Their shivers were no longer a product of the bitter cold that had numbed their limbs; they were shivers brought on by the knowledge that they would not likely survive the endless journey of terror.

Prior to the Indian Removal Act, Jackson's verbiage would become more and more menacing. The American people's patience was being tested to its limits by these prideful, stubborn Natives. Jackson was running out of options.

> Our conduct toward these people is deeply interesting to our national character. Their present condition, contrasted with what they once were, makes a most powerful appeal to our sympathies. Our ancestors found them the uncontrolled possessors of these vast regions. By persuasion and force they have been made to retire from river to river and from mountain to mountain, until some of the tribes have become extinct and others have left but remnants to preserve for awhile their once terrible names. Surrounded by the Whites with their arts of civilization, which by destroying the resources of the savage doom him to weakness and decay, the fate of the Mohegan, the Narragansett, and the Delaware is fast overtaking the Choctaw, the Cherokee, and the Creek. That this fate surely awaits them if they remain within the limits of the states does not admit of a doubt. Humanity and national

honor demand that every effort should be made to avert so great a calamity.
—*Andrew Jackson, December 8, 1829*

Bodies were mutilated and burned; homes built by hand over generations were sending flames and plumes of smoke toward the stars. Those that dropped their futile arms and submitted to the storm of troops were shackled and pressed into lines two wide and hundreds deep as they were led from what had been their home for hundreds of years. All they could do was listen to the fires crackle and the wailing of their loved ones being left behind. Some would not submit to the terrorists that had claimed their land as their own; they paid in blood and pain for their rebellious stance. This was America, just over fifty years after being established as a new world of hope for millions; it was no longer the land of the free—it had become the land of the greedy. Broken spirits began their march across the land with nothing more than the clothes on their backs. The American people's humanity and honor had won the battle over the savages who had done nothing more than live in the homes they had established over many generations—a crime that had become punishable by humiliation, torture, and a gruesome death. The march had begun, the march to a place that was not needed by the American people. Thousands of torturous miles lay ahead of the barefoot and scantily dressed people.

> Toward the aborigines of the country no one can indulge a more friendly feeling than myself, or would go further in attempting to reclaim them from their wandering habits and make them a happy, prosperous people.
> —*Andrew Jackson, December 6, 1830*

The death march raged onward. The Natives were then given a choice: warm themselves with blankets salvaged from nearby smallpox hospitals or freeze to death with the hundreds that had gone before them. On a daily basis, the captives watched dozens drop; the brutality was too much. The cracks of whips were constant; some were put out of their misery with one shot to the head. In many cases, burial was not an option for the fallen; the soldiers could not allow the annoyance of death to stop their progress toward the end goal. People were forced to carry or drag lifeless bodies with them, as the shackles were not always removed when a life ended. In the eyes of the soldiers, carrying loved ones in death or dragging their lifeless body across the ground was an opportunity for the Natives to build character. Smelling the rotting flesh all around them was a time-saving necessity for the soldiers to meet their destination for the week.

> It is pleasing to reflect that results so beneficial, not only to the States immediately concerned, but to the harmony of the Union, will have been accomplished

by measures equally advantageous to the Indians. What the native savages become when surrounded by a dense population and by mixing with the whites may be seen in the miserable remnants of a few Eastern tribes, deprived of political and civil rights, forbidden to make contracts, and subjected to guardians, dragging out a wretched existence, without excitement, without hope, and almost without thought.
—*Andrew Jackson, December 6, 1831*

The removal of the Natives was seen as a resounding success in America. Considered barbarians, they were now heading toward a promising future of living peacefully and civilly alongside American citizens.

The howls and grumbling sounds grew louder and louder as tensions ran to a boiling point with the group. In the darkness, multiple sets of glowing eyes could be seen as the hungry pack of wolves closed in on their helpless prey. The soldiers stopped the train of humanity and began taking bets. Money and laughter was flying in all directions as the rabid animals circled the petrified people. They held one another as best they could and yelled in hopes of scaring the animals away. The people had no strength to protect themselves or one another; many of them looked like skin-covered skeletons. The wolves pounced, ripping the flesh of the unfortunate targets. Screams could be heard for miles—screams of pain and terror; the wolves barked and growled in every direction while protecting their kill. The soldiers laughed as they celebrated the nourishment of the local wildlife. After several minutes of a feeding frenzy, a shot would ring out and the wolves scattered back into the woods. Some would carry what was left of a limb that had been severed from the body of the victim. The animals licked their lips while looking back to make sure nothing edible was left behind; the wolves would do the same before departing. If the victims were still breathing, they would have their heads bashed in with a nearby log or they would be decapitated with an available sharp blade. The last gurgles of choking life would be snuffed out to save bullets.

> After a harassing warfare, prolonged by the nature of the country and by the difficulty of procuring subsistence, the Indians were entirely defeated, and the disaffected band dispersed or destroyed. The result has been creditable to the troops engaged in the service. Severe as is the lesson to the Indians, it was rendered necessary by their unprovoked aggressions, and it is to be hoped that its impression will be permanent and salutary.
> —*Andrew Jackson, December 4, 1832*

The remaining Natives rebelled against the attempts of the American government to lay claim to what was left of their lands in the southern states. Like fishing with dynamite, the drastically outmanned and outgunned Native Americans were destroyed by American soldiers; an example was made for all Native Americans that considered any similar rebellion in the future. The brutality was publicized and spread like wildfire to ensure the Natives understood they had no choice in what was happening all around them. The soldiers destroyed anything they could because all the "unprovoked aggression" had to be snuffed out as quickly as possible in order to protect the American people and their lands. Word was sent of the American victory over the Natives to the human trains that were still traveling west. The frustrated soldiers received word of the rebellion and responded with anger and vengeance.

Children were beaten to death, their body parts strewn along the trail to appease the predators that stalked the train. Women were raped and subsequently met the same fate as the children that were murdered. The trail of body parts and blood ran like a river behind the mass migration. The trails had been established and were visible from great distances; the mayhem that cut through some of the thickest woods in the country was laying a permanent path of sadness across the country.

> My original convictions upon this subject have been confirmed by the course of events for several years, and experience is every day adding to their strength. That those tribes cannot exist surrounded by our settlements and in continual contact with our citizens is certain. They have neither the

intelligence, the industry, the moral habits, nor the desire of improvement that are essential to any favorable change in their condition. Established in the midst of another and a superior race, and without appreciating the causes of their inferiority or seeking to control them, they must necessarily yield to the force of circumstance and ere long disappear.
—*Andrew Jackson, December 3, 1833*

The prophetic words of Andrew Jackson had been proven accurate. The Native Americans refused removal in some cases and fought back, thus being deemed incapable of coexisting with the white settlers of America. There was no other option than to eradicate such a race of people from the land. They were headstrong and were a threat to the development of the United States and its economy. The race of ignorant barbarians had to be removed by any means necessary, or the innocent American people would never survive with any peace of mind. American's had convinced one another they were living among savages that would be a constant threat to their safety and ways of life.

Removal was not enough; the people were to be made to see and believe the same way Americans did. Christianity was the only option; death would follow anyone who dared deny the teachings of the Christian churches. English would be the spoken language, not the languages of uneducated beasts. Again, death would follow if the transformation would not be complete.

Eight

> I regret that the Cherokees east of the Mississippi have not yet determined as a community to remove. How long the personal causes which have heretofore retarded that ultimately inevitable measure will continue to operate I am unable to conjecture. It is certain, however, that delay will bring with it accumulated evils which will render their condition more and more unpleasant. The experience of every year adds to the conviction that emigration, and that alone, can preserve from destruction the remnant of the tribes yet living among us.
> —*Andrew Jackson, December 1, 1834*

A dozen bodies dropped to the frozen ground, heads exploded prior to the collapse of the lifeless corpses. The soldiers lashed out in anger over the struggle the American people endured regarding the movement of the Natives into the western regions. The women cried out as they watched their beloved protectors put to death. They questioned what they as a people had done to deserve such inhumane treatment at the hands of the self-glossed God-fearing intruders. Those that remained could only hope the exodus would conclude soon. They hoped for a quick death; the lengths at which their minds and bodies had abandoned many of them weeks before left them wondering how to end the travesty. The Cherokee people had fought and resisted removal from their lands for years—an unwinnable war had been waged.

They stood strong in the face of the devil, and were inevitably defeated. The defeat would not end in the loss of a battle; it would carry on for months of brutality at the hands of the Americans, and generations would suffer from the memories in the years ahead. A permanent scar was stamped on an entire race of people; the scar was one that could never disappear, no matter what the future held. The government of the United States of America had been given no choice at that point but to use all means available to force the Native people from the lands that needed to be owned and cultivated by Americans. They were left in the unenviable position of conducting genocide in order to develop at its planned rate. That had to be a very difficult position for Jackson to be in; kill them all—God will sort it out. The godless heathens that so rudely stayed in their homes would need to be sent to whatever afterlife they believed in so America could finally move on with its holy growth.

The recognition of the great genocide procured by the US government would be nonexistent when generations of history students were being educated. In those days, it was easy to confuse one another during negotiations. There were language and cultural barriers that were not easily broken down. Because of the barriers, the US government would have its people believe they had no choice but to destroy the threat that the Native Americans posed. They convinced their people that war was the only answer.

I was reminded of a quote that had stuck with me for a very long time.

Make the lie big, make it simple, keep saying it, and eventually they will believe it.

—*Adolf Hitler*

As I wandered the land, the land stained in past atrocities, I could only hold my head in shame for the things my country's forefathers should be accountable for. How could the people trust anyone invading their territory in any fashion? I had so many questions; I wanted badly to lend my mind to unleashing the truth on the world. My small voice would never amount to much, but being able to verbalize the truth that had been stunted for far too long was the least I could do within the project. The Native American people were broken and nearly exterminated; the main person responsible for all of it was rewarded for his bravery and patriotism by having his innocent and brave face pasted on the twenty-dollar bill. The reverence with which our forefathers are spoken of turned my stomach as I saw striking similarities between their words and the words from some of the most evil men in the history of mankind. That realization was as frightening as anything I had encountered in the darkness of our investigations.

NINE

Jason's Walk Begins

BAM! GERALD MIMICKED THE sound, rattled as he told me about the noise from something that had crashed into his house the night before.

I called Gerald to simply discuss some of the things we came across from our first investigation when he told me that things had felt very strange since we left. He said the loud crashing sound had happened before, and he told me it never preceded anything good. Living in the middle of nowhere and having something like that happen in the night would be disturbing to anybody, but Gerald had some level of paranoia to begin with.

"Well, it's Thursday. I will see you a week from Saturday. Are you okay?" I asked him.

"Oh yeah, that is great. Can't wait to see you!" Gerald told me.

I had a meeting set up with Jason Buis a few days before we were scheduled to go, since he would be accompanying me. I wanted to take him so we could have a chance to go through the property and document his unbiased thoughts as we went over everything. Documenting how he felt allowed me to see if it correlated with anything my clients had told me.

"Heck yeah, I can't wait to get down there!" Jason told me with his usual enthusiasm.

"All I can really tell you is we are going to Oklahoma. This is a larger plot of land than anything we have done in the past as far as reports of activity. Other than that, I want to just get your thoughts and feelings and make sure we get it on film." I explained the very basics to him as we finalized our plans for the upcoming weekend. I made sure not to include any details about the Allen brothers, the history of the region, the reports of activity, or the events that occurred when Jeremiah and I were there.

Saturday morning rolled around and Jason and I were determined to get an early start. Jason seemed a little less enthusiastic that morning than he did the other night when we had set our plans.

"You okay, bro?" I asked him.

"Yeah, had some strange dreams since we talked though, but I'm good. This place must be crazy; something has been in my head ever since we talked," he told me.

"We'll be fine, dude, but it is active. I wouldn't take you somewhere to waste your time," I reminded Jason.

"Ha! Yeah, I figured as much. We need to be careful though—this place is strong. I don't usually get vivid warnings and visions before I even see a place. I've had dreams about so many energies down there, but I can't put my finger on everything. I'm looking forward to it, but this place is nuts, I can already tell!" he told me as we finished packing up our gear.

After about three hours, I noticed he got noticeably quiet and seemed to be distant. I turned up the music to let ourselves find our thoughts.

We reached Oklahoma, and it wasn't long before we were on the winding roads in the hills, surrounded by the beautiful scenery and eerie surroundings that came with it.

We were a little ways from the property when Jason opened up about a few things.

"There is something about a 'hanging tree.' I can hear a voice talking about it as they point in its direction. So I know the land has seen tragedy, not just through its history, but pretty recent. I also get the feeling there are unmarked graves, at least three of them. I feel like they are children that have been buried near a house on the property," he told me, and then continued, "I'm seeing something about hostile little creatures, or little people. It's really weird, almost like small people that are hostile toward those that inhabit the land. They may actually be, or possibly are tied to, extraterrestrials," Jason told me as he tried to remain focused.

"Anything else?" I asked. It was always amazing to me to witness his level of intuition.

"Yeah, I feel a lot of energy, but the details are real murky. Every few minutes I feel dizziness and I just know there is a lot more to it, I just can't see it clearly," he finished his thought.

We took the long, slow drive down the back road as we finally made it to the Allen property. Marvin and Annette were already there piling up wood for the bonfire they had planned for the evening. They greeted us with huge smiles and hugs.

I introduced Jason to them and reminded them we wanted to keep everything about the property quiet until he had a chance to do his walk-through.

"Oh yeah, we were just finishing up preparations. We'll have supper and a fire going later," Marvin told us, "We are going to head out so you guys can do what you need to do. Gerald is in town right now; he shouldn't be back until later."

"I appreciate it, Marvin, and thank you, Annette. You guys are awesome; the place looks great, Marvin!" I said, noticing the work he had done to tend the overgrowth. The thick bushes and grass had been manicured. The abandoned house was a simple walk now; we wouldn't have to chop our way through the thick brush.

After finding out that Gerald had spent the week in New Mexico at the funeral of a relative, my thoughts went back to what he had told me about the banging sound. He had told me that the banging sound had previously foreshadowed bad things to come.

I started gathering up the equipment and made sure I was ready to roll as Jason took a little stroll around.

"You okay?" I asked him.

"Yeah, this place is amazing. I don't know what it is, but there is something different here, different than I think I've ever felt before," he told me. "The whole place feels like one big burial ground," he said to my surprise. That happened to be my reaction the second I got out of the car when Jeremiah and I had first arrived.

I allowed Jason to wander a little bit while I was getting everything ready. I recalled the talk we had about the owl before our first investigation and the fact that they bring with them spirit activity, which seemed to be the case on that first night following the call of the owl. Now this—something large seemed to loom over the land. It seemed to make sure every living person around knew that there would be signs and that they should not be ignored.

Jason and I made our way to the abandoned shack. My camera was fixed on Jason's every move. He slowly made his way toward a large tree that stood about twenty feet in front of the side opening to the house, and he stopped.

"There are unmarked graves. I feel drawn toward this tree; I think there is something right around here, probably two of them. Something is also drawing me toward the backyard area. I want to look in the back before we go in," Jason told me.

I had brought my dowsing rods for that exact purpose. In theory, dowsing rods are able to lead you to energy sources that may be coming from the land. When there is a location of interest, the rods will naturally cross themselves with what feels like a magnetic pull on each rod. The rods are supposed to lead the user to unmarked graves, water sources, metal sources, and other things of that nature when used properly. I went to where Jason felt the energy, and sure enough, several times I was stopped by the crossing of my dowsing rods. We marked each location for further investigation later on.

My mind wandered to the first night's investigation—*"Look in back!"* I remembered the forceful voice over the walkie-talkie.

As we reached the rear of the house, we paused at the tree line and Jason looked deep into the woods.

"I think there are more unmarked graves here, maybe just one, but I feel a child close by. I don't feel any communication. There is hesitation. There are eyes everywhere, not just on us, they are on everybody," Jason said. He looked in all directions as he slowly made his way around to the west side of the house.

"That room is significant," Jason continued as he pointed to the window that led to the side of the house, "I see faces peering into that room from out there, something very mischievous and bitter. There are more than one, but I am not positive—I think two or three. They look in and watch the horrible things that go on in there and enjoy it. They also try to make things happen to people. They cackle. Creepy," he told me. I was stunned. Jason had described the witches that had been seen many times peering into the window over the years.

"We are not welcome here; nobody is," he told me.

We made our way back to the opposite side of the house so we could enter. Jason paused before we entered through the side of the house, "This was not accidental, I don't care what anybody says," he said, in reference to the burned portion of the house.

"Not an accident, huh?" I asked.

"Not at all. The house took what it saw as an opportunity to cleanse the land that has been defiled. The house wanted to burn down. It's as though it is alive and living with the past. The past on this land goes back as long as time and it is drenched in negativity," he told me.

We proceeded to make our way into the house. Our steps were delicate since the floorboards had proven to be brittle. We made our way into the kitchen area and Jason walked slowly toward "the Room of Faces." "I don't really want to go in that room right this second," he told me and paused.

"Let's go in there," he pointed across the hall into the back room. We made our way across the hallway, dodging the broken boards.

"The environment in here is extremely oppressive; someone could go mad spending too much time in here. Suicidal thoughts come to mind almost immediately," Jason explained, standing in the middle of the room. I was in the hallway with my camera pointed in.

"What is in here that is so oppressive?" I asked Jason.

"The entire house is oppressive. There is so much negative energy in here, and it's hard to say where it originates or if one portion of the house is any safer than any other. No wonder they left; nobody should live here. This is a cesspool of negative energy," he finished his thought. I made my way into the room as he stepped back closer to the doorway.

Just as Jason reached the entry to the room, he paused as he clutched his head with his hands, "Ahhh, damn!"

"What's wrong?" I asked him. He seemed shaken.

"I just felt like—an explosion of energy right around here. Damn, that hurt," he told me. He was standing within feet of the spot where Gerald said the huge glass explosion had taken place on Christmas Day.

"Dang, dude, is it gone? You okay?" I asked him.

"Yeah, I'm fine, that was crazy! That rattled my whole head. I've never felt anything that strong before. I just felt a huge boom," he said as we made our way across the hall and into the kitchen.

"Dude, that's pretty awesome," I told him, as I continued to explain what Gerald had reported. I also let him know that was the final incident before they had abandoned the house.

"Holy crap! I don't blame them! That was nuts. I don't think the boom came from the kitchen, though; I think it came from Gerald's room," he said while we made our way to the Room of Faces.

I was in awe of the similarities that Jason had provided when compared to what the Allen brothers had told us. We entered the Room of Faces; I insisted because I needed to know what Jason thought about the room.

"There is so much emotion throughout the house: sadness, hatred, it's just a lot. This is intense," Jason said. We kept working our way through the house, "I feel like I want to cry. I can't explain it, but I just feel like I want to cry," he continued.

We entered the Room of Faces and almost immediately, Jason began to breathe erratically. He seemed weak.

"What is it?" I asked him.

"Dang, something just came after me. What the hell?" he told me.

"Something attacked you?" I asked as he nodded.

"The mirror, something is bad about the mirror. Reflections of negativity, faces in the window right there, just like I saw outside. They look in and try to send harmful things in to hurt people," he said.

"Crazy, dude, can you see what happens?" I was digging for more information.

"Rape, mental anguish, and torture—the dark energies come through here and try to hurt people. I'm seeing the little creatures again; they try to harm whoever is in here. The faces, it seems like they were human once, but not everything in here was. Nobody could live here for long without going crazy," he told me. We made our way back into the kitchen.

The energy throughout the small house was palpable. I was feeling a very hard pressure in my ears at that point. We made our way toward the living room area. I had felt that pressure every time I had been in the house; it always seemed to go away after I left the house. At that point, I was ready to finish up that portion of the walk and move on. I was starting to get dizzy.

"Geez," Jason continued as he stepped into the living room, "children were tormented in this house for a long time. I feel like Gerald and Marvin both would have been tormented, but Marvin drew in a particularly dark energy," he told me as he looked around.

"Yeah, that is familiar too, so spit it out—not everything in this house has been human, right? Demonic?" I asked.

"Yup, and the floor collapsing wasn't a coincidence either. When you all were walking through last time, the floor falling was an attempt for the house to get you out of here," he told me. I hadn't mentioned the floor collapsing to him. I had a very difficult time thinking the living room floor, already warped, didn't just collapse because of our weight. I struggled to call it a sign, but I was intrigued because I hadn't mentioned it at all to Jason. I chalked it up to something we would never know for sure.

Jason then looked down and fell into a panic. "All right, we need to go, let's go," he told me as he walked quickly into the kitchen and almost bowled me over on his way by.

"What is it?" I asked, trying to get him to stop to explain.

"Dude, what the hell?" I asked him as I met up with him outside.

"That knife on the floor of the living room, I don't know what it is, I felt like one of us was about to be stabbed with it," he told me, regaining his breath.

"I had noticed the knife, but nobody had really pointed it out as relevant. I thought it was just another piece of junk," I told him.

"I don't like it; I just saw it in my mind's eye flying at us. Not cool," he said.

"All right, well, you have been pretty much dead-on with everything you felt in there. They told us almost the exact same stories you just told me. I'm not going to deny what you feel, but don't think for a second that we aren't going to try to use that knife later as a trigger object," I told him, only partly in jest.

"Ha! Right, jerk," he told me as we both chuckled.

TEN

Jason's Walk Concludes

Was that you?" I asked Jason as we were chatting outside the house.

"Um, not sure what you mean," he replied.

We heard a low grumbling sound again, and more persistent. The second time clearly came from inside the house.

"That!" I told him and began to scramble back into the house to see what might be the source of the growl. As I was entering the house, I didn't know if I would rather find the source or not, but I needed to get back in and make sure our recorder was still rolling.

"That was loud! The recorder is running; no way did it not catch that," I told Jason.

"Crazy!" Jason said.

After a few minutes of unsuccessfully coaxing whatever made the noise, we made our way back outside to finish the walk. The review of our audio files following the night's investigation would prove that not only was there some type of disembodied growl, but it happened two times. It was also accompanied by the faint sound of a menacing chuckle.

Jason and I made our way down the long driveway toward Gerald's house. We walked through the area of the yard where another structure used to stand. Jason noted that there could still be energy hanging out near the old location, as it used to be very active when the house stood.

"Whatever was here is still here. I think it bothers Gerald sometimes in his house. It goes everywhere on the property," Jason told me, standing where the house once did.

We continued to walk toward Gerald's house when Jason stopped, looked up, and said, "This is the hanging tree. I get a bad vibe from this tree, bad energy. Something still hangs out in this tree and spies on people."

"Damn, dude," was all I could muster. Jason was standing just below the branch that we were told the Allen brothers' uncle hung himself from.

We continued our walk around the perimeter of Gerald's house; Jason noted that he was definitely interested in what might be going on inside the house.

"What is with all the banging noises? It's like some creatures just roam around the land and bang on things with large objects! I hear it all over the place; it sounds like wood cracking against wood," Jason told me. He mentioned the fact that he could tell the banging sound happened in these houses, not just in the surrounding woods.

"This place is crazy; I can't keep up with it. There is just too much going on to keep up with; it's making me dizzy!" Jason said with a chuckle. We were both exhausted and we hadn't even begun the actual investigation yet.

Shortly after we completed the walk-through of the property, Gerald showed up with a friend of his and introduced us.

"Hey fellas! Thanks for coming back down. I guess we didn't scare you away!" Gerald said as he laughed hysterically.

"This is my very good friend, Mark," Gerald said, and Jason and I said hello to Mark.

We reviewed some of the things that had been going on. Gerald, being a natural storyteller, was happy to tell us even more stories. We discussed the caves and let Gerald know we were planning to head down there before the sun went down.

"I'll take you guys down there. I could show you some things and tell you a little about the history," Mark said. We made our way to the other side of the fence and began the long hike down into the canyon of woods toward the caves.

We all made our way across the creek and did our best not to break a limb in the process. The rocks and running water made it a very slippery trek to the entrance of two main caves that hid within the belly of the cliffs. Mark was telling us about the water demons.

"The person would disappear. It is told that the body would be pulled into the water and the soul removed from the body before the demon would inhabit the physical body and return as the person. Within two weeks, the person would appear to die of sickness, so it would be nearly impossible for anyone to know what really happened to the person," Mark said, watching the waters of the creek pass us by.

"So they would show back up as the person even though the person was already gone? Like a human costume?" I asked.

"Yeah, pretty spooky. That's why we leave offerings whenever we come down here, usually tobacco," Mark said, so we all sprinkled some tobacco into the running water.

The three of us climbed up into the large opening to one of the caves that extended deep into the cliff. Mark told us several stories, including the James gang having been known to frequent the caves in the area as hiding places. The caves had been mystical monuments for a very long time in the eyes of the Cherokee. Mark explained some theories that the little people originated in the caves and had an underground tunnel system that ran under the entire area.

"I remember coming down here when I was little one morning and couldn't believe what I saw. We were in the middle of a really bad drought, so the creek had all but dried up during the summer. One morning when I came down here, there were waterfalls flowing from the sides of these cliffs. Water was pouring from countless openings of the cliff side. The creek had begun to flow again, but the waterfalls only lasted for about two hours. There never was any logical explanation as to what may have caused them. I've never seen anything like it since then," Mark explained.

It was very easy to get sucked into the stories of these people, as most of them were kept very quiet within their community.

It would be pitch-black soon, so we decided to start our hike back. Jason and I were appreciative that Mark took the time to show us the caves and tell us some of the local legends that came along with them.

Mark had been a caretaker for Gerald, not just a friend. He lived with Gerald for a while when he was sick a couple years prior. Gerald had been scared of what might happen on the land, so he asked Mark to help him conjure some type of protector. It had long been known throughout history that different tribes would quarrel between their own small faction or family and sometimes others within their own tribe. The disputes would oftentimes turn very bloody and bitter. Mark told us about the fact that both good and bad medicine was something still practiced throughout the Cherokee culture.

"I like to believe that it happens less now than it used to be, but it used to be really common. It was so frequent that if you would just look at someone the wrong way, if they were powerful enough, they could cause all kinds of harm—from misfortune, to sickness, even death," Mark told us.

"Lands were cursed quite often, there didn't have to be a good reason for it. Some Indians were just mean and in some ways, as a form of entertainment, they would commonly cast spells and curses on their enemy's families and lands. The witches used to cast spells and curses a lot; that's what happened here," Mark continued.

"Gerald was sick and afraid; he wouldn't go outside, especially at night. He knew about the curse, so he asked me to help him conjure a protector," he said.

"So you helped him conjure protection to combat whatever had been brought on the land that was negative? I assume these are not human spirits," I asked.

"No, not human at all. After every meal, the families would leave a small portion for the demons and hope that it would keep them at bay. It would work a lot of times, but other times the demons would lash out. They had been called on to wreak havoc on the land and the people that inhabit the land, so offerings did not always help. We conjured a protector outside of Gerald's house to try to keep him separated from all the dark spirits that roam the property. Every corner of the property has had something conjured, so everything inside the land is vulnerable to whatever might be out there. These spirits can take on many forms. They can appear as people, they can appear as animals, anything. It doesn't really matter. It is dark and nearly impossible to fix," Mark continued his story. "A lot of times, if you die on the property, you are bound here because the demons collect souls. They will not let the soul pass on to the spirit world—they trap them."

We stood quietly listening to Mark.

"Yes, this is a powerful place," Mark said, "I couldn't stay here because it was wearing me down. I have always been pretty sensitive to certain things and I felt like I was marked in a way. I couldn't live here longer than I did. I was sure it would be the death of me and no way would I die here," he finished.

We arrived back at the property and Gerald, Marvin, and Annette were putting the final touches on the bonfire for the evening before setting it ablaze.

"Are you guys ready to go check out Manus? That place will blow your mind. Nobody likes going there during the day, let alone at night," Gerald told us. I began to feel butterflies in my stomach. Manus Cemetery was a place Jeremiah and I were told about during the last trip.

"Hell yes, let's go. Anyone else going?" I asked as Jason and I gathered our things.

Gerald had agreed to take us over there, and Mark agreed to go as well. We all had some level of concern about spending time at Manus due to the stories of powerful entities being commonplace there. The four of us packed up the car and headed out as Marvin and Annette stayed behind to make dinner and start a warm fire.

We drove for a couple miles; the cemetery was close to the Allen property, but there wasn't a quick way to access it without driving. We pulled onto another meandering dirt road and made our way back farther into nowhere. We noticed a few abandoned houses along the way that certainly set the scene for a creepy venture. Once we turned, we drove about a quarter of a mile and we pulled in to park. The cemetery was rather small, but it could be felt in our core.

The fence surrounding the cemetery was ominous; there were two entry arches that held the name of Manus on them and seemed less than welcoming to visitors. Thick woods surrounded the place and there were two trees within the actual cemetery. They were both large, they were intimidating, and they commanded attention and respect. The back of the cemetery looked to the west; the trees grew on the north and south sides close to the entrance on the east side. In the distance to the west we could see what looked like a functional house; it was at least a half-mile or more in the distance.

I stood separate from everyone in awe of the overwhelming place. I could feel the energy immediately. I had been to countless cemeteries in the past, but this one had a feel to it like no other I had experienced.

"Dang, this is crazy," Jason said.

"You be careful in here now, you understand? Try not to step on any of the gravestones and walk carefully. People don't come here because they get followed home. It happens all the time," Gerald told us.

Jason and I took note of the warning Gerald had provided. We knew there would be no taunting or pushing the spirits to communicate; I could tell that would not be necessary. There was something there, and I would be much more surprised if it didn't communicate with us than if it did. We walked through the entrance and got a few steps inside when Mark paused.

"Nah, I'm not going. I can't. I don't feel right," he told us as he made his way back toward the car.

With each step we took, it was as though at any moment we could step right into a grave and sink like quicksand. The ground was some of the softest I had ever felt beneath my feet. We were walking on solid land covered with grass; it was bone dry, yet it felt like something could reach up from below and pull us down into whatever dimension might lie beneath us. It was a terrifying place. I could easily see why Mark turned back. I noticed Jason moving slowly and struggling a little bit.

"You okay?" I asked him.

"Yeah, but this place is strong. There are almost always watchers at cemeteries, but something else is here. Either there are a lot of them or there is something totally different and way more powerful. Watch your back," he told me.

Gerald walked around and kept reiterating how creepy the place was. Several times he brought me over to where he was so he could point out the final resting place of a family member. A lot of the Allen family had been laid to rest there. Despite the undeniable frightening feeling the location oozed, there was serenity to it as well.

"You hear that?" I asked Jason.

"What?" Jason replied.

"You hear how hard the wind is blowing? I don't feel a thing, not even a breeze. What the hell is going on?" I continued.

"You're right," he agreed.

The wind was howling all around the location, but we were not feeling so much as a whisper of wind on our faces within the confines of the cemetery. Very thick woods on all sides except the entrance side encircled the place, so the woods could provide a cover and knock the wind down to a crawl before breaching the cemetery.

"You came!" [RT-EVP]

"Huh?" I asked as I looked over at Jason.

"What?" Jason looked back at me.

"Did you just say something?" I continued.

"Nope, not a word," Jason confirmed.

I knew without a doubt that I just heard a voice in my ear as we slowly crept toward the back of the cemetery. I verbally marked it on my recorder so I could review it later. I was wearing headphones, so everything I was hearing was on a two-second delay from when it was actually happening.

I was snapping pictures and slowly making my way around the perimeter.

"Here! Come here!" Gerald told me. I made my way over to him.

"Mary Dreadfulwater—who is that?" I asked him.

"She was one of the meanest bitches around. She was a witch! A wicked witch!" Gerald told me. He unknowingly started taking slow steps backward and suddenly had a frightened look on his face.

"Fear, die, go now." [RT-EVP]

"Jesus!" I said as I backed away from the stone. I had heard a clear voice, one that sounded cracking yet feminine. I took it as a sign.

"You want us to leave?" I asked.

"GO!" [RT-EVP]

An immediate response came through my ear so clearly that I almost snatched the earphones from my ears. I jumped back naturally; Gerald and I decided it might be a good time to take ourselves back toward the car. We confirmed what we had come here to confirm: Manus seemed to be extremely active. We would surely return.

"Here, Brandon, this is another one of the witches that my mother knew. Minnie Cotine used to know my mother, but she would also practice bad medicine too. When you have the gift of medicine, you should never use it on people in a negative way. She ended up burning alive in her cabin just a mile or so down the road from our property," Gerald explained some of the background of the witch.

"Wow, it is incredible the evil that people can put on each other. Do you believe Minnie and Mary are still around in spirit?" I asked Gerald.

"Oh, hell yes! They would be two of the witches that are seen all over the place. We used to see these ugly witches peering into the house from outside. It scared me to death! These two evil ladies would definitely still be around," Gerald said.

"Damn, that place is for real," Jason said as he peeked over his shoulder. He jumped and panicked, "Holy, what the—" Jason hustled into the open door of the car and slammed it shut.

I looked back in the direction where he was startled and noticed nothing, but I believed I heard some type of shuffling in close proximity to where he had been looking.

As the doors to the car shut, I asked Jason what happened.

"Something rushed me, it was crazy. I don't know what it was, but I felt like we were in serious danger just then," he said.

"Yeah, that place is legit," I said with a lighter tone, hoping to break some of the tension that had built up in the car. Gerald laughed, Jason nervously chuckled, and Mark just continued to look out the window as we left the cemetery behind in a cloud of dust kicked up by the tires.

We arrived back at the property to meet up with Annette and Marvin. They had the fire blazing and a table full of food waiting for us. We noted Manus Cemetery as a definite place of interest, considering the ties to the family and land. I had visions of the witches making their way through the woods as they pleased to visit the property they had allegedly tormented for years during their lives. We all took a few deep breaths and parked the car. Annette and Marvin greeted us as we headed toward the table to grab something to eat.

"B, grab the recorder. Let's go over there," Jason pointed toward the hanging tree down near Gerald's house.

"You see that? Right there in the tree," Jason pointed as I shook my head.

"What the hell is it?" I asked Jason, as I began to take some pictures in the direction he was pointing.

"I'm not completely sure; it looks like a shadow person or what would normally be a watcher of some sort," he told me. "It's up there watching all of us," he continued.

"Can you say something? Who are you watching?" I asked.

"You." *[EVP immediate response]*

"Hello?" I inquired.

"*Go. Please.*" [EVP]

"Do you have your RT-EVP on you right now?" Jason asked me.

"I just turned it on. I'm about to put the earphones in. Why?" I replied.

"I think you may have just got a response," he told me.

Marvin and Annette joined us by the tree as our line of questioning continued for several minutes. There was a constant feeling of being watched throughout the property. I was not sure if the feeling stemmed from whatever Jason had his eyes on in the tree or if it came from another place. There was an uneasy feeling to the air that evening, although that seemed to be more and more typical as my time there went by.

I decided to head into the house while Jason, Marvin, and Annette continued discussing the creature Jason had spotted in the tree. Something was drawing me into the house, so I felt like I needed to go in.

"So here I am, I'm all alone. Is there anything you have to say to me?" I called into the darkness.

"Can you tell me your purpose in being here?" I continued.

"*I can kill, if I crave.*" [EVP]

I could feel the air getting thicker as the pressure built inside my head. I continued my line of questioning. I could hear Jason approaching from the outside, as many of the windows in the house had been broken out over the course of time.

Jason joined me in the house and we crept from room to room continuing our investigation.

"I just feel completely overwhelmed. I can't really focus. I feel like something keeps coming at me," he told me.

A metallic sounding growl occurred. [Disembodied sound]

"What the—" Jason stammered.

"Did you hear that?" I asked him as we both swung our heads toward the back of the house.

"Um, yeah, I've never heard anything like that," Jason said.

"It was like some kind of robot or something!" I confirmed. I started to make my way toward the location I thought the noise had come from.

"Who are you? Was that you growling at us?" I asked.

Laughing. [Disembodied sound]

I almost fell backward as I heard the laugh coming from the back room. I hesitated to move forward to enter, as I was both scared to death of what I might find and worried about the reliability of the crumbling floors in the room.

"Did you hear that?" I asked Jason. He stood in the kitchen near the entry to the living room.

"What? I just heard the growling a minute ago," he said.

"There was laughing back here; it had to get picked up by the recorder. It was clear as day," I informed him.

We continued looking around for several more minutes. The house seemed to go quiet following the feeling of intimidation that had been seared into our hearts and minds.

Jason and I decided that we would leave some equipment rolling in the house as we went back out to meet up with Marvin, Annette, and Gerald. They were gathered around the campfire. As Jason and I made our way out of the house and toward the fire, we quietly discussed the fact that the place was littered with all kinds of energy, and it was intent on taking all of ours with it. Feeling completely drained of energy, we sat down with our friends by the fire. They pointed out that exhaustion was written all over our faces.

"You boys need to be careful in there. This stuff doesn't play around," Gerald told us.

"You're telling me. It's crazy. I can barely stand up right now," I let my guard down a little as the warmth of the fire wrapped us like a blanket.

ELEVEN

Gerald the Storyteller

WE ALL SAT AROUND the fire exchanging stories of our past and sharing our experiences that evening. The comfort level between us all had grown considerably. Jason and I took turns telling them about our evening, and we took our friends to our past with us as we recounted stories from previous investigations we had conducted over the years. Having grown up in a very spiritual place, Marvin, Annette, and Gerald were able to tell us many stories that had been handed down over many generations. I explained my theories about the significance of ley lines and informed them that we were sitting in the middle of one of the densest clusters of intersecting lines the United States had to offer.

"I don't doubt that to be true at all. There has always been significance in geography in Native American culture," Gerald told us.

"The Trail of Tears actually followed very closely to the ley lines that lead from the originating point in North Carolina all the way across the country on the path that was taken to get here. It ends with several intersecting points here in the Tahlequah area. I don't know that it was necessarily by design, but according to the maps I use, that is the case," I explained.

"Tahlequah has always been a very spiritual place. It doesn't surprise me a bit to hear that there may be other powers at work that led the Cherokee Nation here," Gerald said.

"Brandon, will you come with me? I would like to talk to you," Gerald asked me to take a walk with him.

We made our way down the driveway to his house, he opened the door, and I followed him in. The place was rough to say the least. Gerald was comforted by his dogs; he kept quite a few of them in his small house with him. He had trouble getting around, so the house was in pretty bad shape. I ignored the mess and sat down to talk to my friend.

"We have formed a great friendship already, Brandon; I have relied on intuition all my life. I know people and I can always tell when I connect with them very quickly. I am sick, I don't know how long I will be here, but you all are here for a reason and it gives me peace," he told me. "You all will continue to investigate this place, because it needs to happen. The stories of our people and this land need to be told, and your heart brought you here, and you are here to stay."

I took Gerald's words to heart because it was as though he was looking into my soul. He knew my desire to learn as much as I possibly could, and he understood that everything going on around us was educating us more and more by the minute.

"I want you all to come down here anytime, even if you aren't coming to work and investigate. We want you to come down and just enjoy this land with us. You never know what is going to pop up, but it's a case where we know what is here. Whether you all find it or not doesn't matter to us because we know it's here. It has been here far longer than my people and has grown in strength since the arrival of my people. You all are family now. You are welcome here anytime. Whatever is here isn't going anywhere, which is a fact. There have been things far beyond our understanding that have been called to this place; they manifest in many different ways, but Tahlequah and our home is now a part of you," Gerald continued.

I sat in complete understanding of the warnings he had imparted when we first arrived. I could feel this majestic place working its way into my soul more and more by the minute. I was mesmerized by it.

"There is a big infiltration of spirits, ghosts, demons, and whatnot. There's lots of sorcery. My dad, like Marvin told you, was Catholic and then became a Southern Baptist minister. Well, about twenty-five years ago, before he passed away, he was invited to a place," Gerald's voice was hesitant as he continued his recollection. "It was not a reservation but a community of many Cherokee families. This girl there had become possessed and there was a group of elders, spiritual leaders of the community, that had got together to try to help this girl. She was a young girl at the time. I was told stories of this girl's voice changing, her face transformed into a demon—she had been completely taken over. The voices from the girl came in three different voices, all of which spoke different languages. The spiritual leaders spent day and night for weeks trying to rid this poor girl of the demon that had gotten inside her. Eventually, the demon was expelled, but the idea of something like that happening to a child really affected all of us," Gerald told me in a somber voice.

"Years later, Marvin had gone off to college at Haskell, up in Lawrence, Kansas," he continued. "He met this girl, Melissa, and he and she were fooling around in his truck on one of the dirt roads back there," he told us.

"Her eyes all of a sudden turned red, and she began speaking in tongues, languages like he had never heard before in his life. Marvin struggled to get out of the truck and he took off! We found out later that it was Melissa that had been the little girl that had been possessed when we were children. This is when I realized there truly is pure evil out there and it takes no prisoners," Gerald looked down and paused. It was a story he had kept to himself for a very long time. He was telling me a story about Marvin's experience that Marvin had not yet been comfortable enough to share on his own.

"I live here alone, Brandon, and since Mark moved out last fall, I have lived in total fear. I sleep during the day; I stay awake all night long. I'm just scared to death; I wish someone lived here with me. I don't know what is out here, but there is something and I feel like I am in danger all the time. Everyone is afraid of this land, they really don't spend much time out here, it's just a spooky place." Gerald was trying to keep himself on track at that point.

"I sleep with one eye open it seems. I have guns and knives all over this house, not because I necessarily think they will do much good against whatever is around here, but they do make me feel somewhat protected," he continued.

"I have prayer and I have my faith. It's what we all need in our lives. I am Catholic, and I do believe that I am protected by God. I see on the news about the devastating tsunamis and earthquakes going on all over the world—there is a shift happening right now, and we all need to hold onto our faith," he told me.

I spoke to Gerald about some of the things Jeremiah and I had experienced during our last trip, as he hadn't been around much to go over all that had happened.

"I haven't told you about a lot of the things that my mother told me happened here when she was growing up. There was so much witchcraft, black magic, and bad medicine practiced around here, it was a dangerous place. In many ways it still is because a lot of the old ways are still in place. They just aren't spoken about much. Curses on land and people were and are very common when it comes to this way of life," he told me. A lot of his thoughts reiterated the stories Mark had told Jason and me earlier in the evening.

"The demons of this land are mean, they are vengeful, and if they haven't been fed, then they lash out. They have sexually assaulted almost every member of my family at some point. Both of our older brothers told us about it happening to them. My grandmother and mother both told us about the demon that lives in that house," Gerald gestured to the abandoned house.

"It has lived on this land longer than we have. It has been in that house for a very long time," he told me.

I explained to Gerald the fact that in my past I had also been assaulted by a dark force that I could not explain. It was a connection that we had made; I hadn't told anybody about the assault to that point, other than my closest friends and coworkers.

"That is crazy! That thing over there is alive, the house seems like it is alive, and it has haunted our family for generations. It's the scariest thing in the world, what lives in that house over there. It's real. There is no denying it. It can do whatever it wants to anybody at any time—you can't see it and it is very hard to protect yourself against it if it lashes out at you. There really is no escaping it. There are processes that you can do, ritualistic things that can help protect you, but it is complicated, it is difficult to do," Gerald's voice began to tail off.

"There was a time when there were rituals performed at the water's edge down there," Gerald pointed in the direction of the creek down below. "They would use their devices to conduct their ritual, and it is said that whoever may be performing bad medicine on someone would appear in the water. I feel bad because I feel like I am exposing you guys to more than you may be able to take. Please don't forget, this shit is very powerful. People shouldn't be exposed to the things you will be exposed to down here. Please keep your faith and God close and make sure you don't allow the darkness to get into your heart. I just want to make sure you understand the seriousness of this place," Gerald explained.

"This place will quickly become a part of you. The spirits will get to know you; they probably knew you were coming before you even got here. They knew you before we did. It's crazy!" Gerald laughed.

"What are those? They are so neat," I stood up and walked over to a glass case that housed a lot of artifacts. There were several small figurines that caught my eye, as well as what looked like a very old Native American knife.

"Oh, Brandon, those are old. They have been passed down through generations. Those are actually Mark's kachina dolls. Keep the glass closed," Gerald told me with a serious tone.

"Why keep the glass closed?" I asked him.

"Because those objects are drenched in energy, both good and bad. If they were to be removed from the glass, my house, already being very active, would very likely be even worse. A lot of those figurines were used almost like voodoo dolls by medicine men and women many years ago. The energy that clings to them seems to be mostly contained when they are in the glass case. If they were taken out, I don't know what would happen. Probably nothing good," Gerald laughed.

"They are beautiful, incredible stuff," I told him as he nodded. "You know, I would be happy to bring the equipment in here as well if you'd like me to try to figure out what may be here."

"One day, just not today. You and me both know that communicating with these things can lead to other things. While I am living here, I would rather not," Gerald told me. I agreed with him, knowing that if they had still lived in the other house, our approach would have been much different. We opened the door back up and headed back to the fire where our friends were still sitting.

As the night grew long, Jason and I began packing up the equipment. It had been a long and emotional night for both of us. We said our farewells to Annette and the Allen brothers and drove down the maze of dirt roads into the pitch-black of the night. We made the long journey home; Jason was asleep before we hit the highway. We had a few minutes to discuss our thoughts as we arrived back in town just as the sun was beginning to come over the horizon. The place seemed to become a part of us from the minute we had arrived. I found it difficult to believe that it wouldn't become a part of anybody that went down there with an open mind. It was incredible.

TWELVE

Home Sweet Home

IN THE DAYS FOLLOWING our trip to Oklahoma, life went on as usual. Spring was about to give way to the hot summer months. I was in regular contact with Marvin, Gerald, and Annette. We would check in with one another just to say hello and see how things were going. One afternoon my phone rang—Marvin's number showed up on the caller ID.

"Hey man, how's it going down there?" I greeted him.

"It's crazy; activity around here has been picking up a lot lately. No doubt something to do with what we've been doing," he told me.

"Oh yeah? What's been going on?" I asked.

"I woke up today with some scratches on my arm. I have also woke up for no reason at 3:33 a.m. for the past several nights," he explained.

"Scratches? Are they deep? Any way you may have caught your arm on something and just not remembered?" I asked.

"Nah, my nails are pretty much nonexistent, and when I woke up, my arm started burning. That's when I noticed them. I'm sure I didn't hit my arm on anything. I'm all right, it was just scary," he said.

"I'll bet! That's crazy. Can you send me a picture?" I was hoping to document the occurrence.

"Yup, I'll send them to you shortly. I have been hearing a lot of knocking on my place too; usually it comes and goes, always in sets of three though. That's mostly it, but when I was out doing yard work to get ready for this weekend, I felt like something was watching me from inside the house," he said.

I asked Marvin if he was sure he wanted to continue the project and he confirmed he did. We discussed the importance of documenting everything as it happened. I would be heading back down a few days later.

Immediately after we got off the phone, I got in touch with my brother, Courtney (a.k.a. Snort), as well as Jason Buis and another friend, Jared. I had to let them know what was going on. I had to question whether or not we were all safe—the answer was beginning to feel like a resounding "no," but I had filled everyone in on all the risks and details of what had been experienced. Everybody had the door wide open to stop at any time. This went beyond a typical case—it had become a project with no end in sight.

The four of us and Snort's wife, Jenn, would get together that evening to discuss the upcoming weekend.

I was getting ready to take a shower before heading over to their house for dinner when suddenly the lights over the vanity area outside the bathroom began flickering. They both went out completely for about thirty seconds. They came back on as I stood frozen, wondering what was going on. The house was new—there were no electrical issues. I was prepared to grab more light bulbs when the lights came back on as if nothing had happened.

BOOM! BOOM! BOOM!

I almost jumped headfirst through the mirror in front of me as three loud bangs came from the bathroom door just behind me. My heart nearly came through my chest as I swung around to face the door; I suddenly felt like I was being watched, just as I had felt down in Oklahoma. I slowly reached out to the knob on the bathroom door and opened the door. As it creaked open, I flipped on the light switch as I made my way into the bathroom. The feeling of being watched lifted. I took a few deep breaths and convinced myself I had just experienced some strange coincidences and should move on. I finished getting ready and headed to my brother's house, still wondering what the hell just happened.

Everyone arrived at Jenn and Snort's house around the same time. We gathered outside in the backyard where the grill was burning hot and the smell of barbecue was thick in the air.

"Oh shit! Are you serious?" Jared said as I finished telling them about what had happened.

"Dead serious, it was insane," I confirmed.

"They already followed you home?" Snort said. He was very excited to get a chance to check the place out.

"I don't know if something necessarily followed me home, but there were a couple really weird things that happened within a minute of each other. It scared the hell out of me, that's for sure. The strange thing about it was all of it happened just a few minutes after speaking to Marvin about all the activity going on down there," I told them.

"That place is crazy. I don't doubt that there will be energy with us as we come home; it's everywhere down there and could probably travel easily," Jason said.

We all continued our talks as we finished up dinner. We talked for a while about how life was and planned everything for our next trip to Oklahoma.

As I was driving home, my phone rang; I saw that it was Marvin's number, so I answered as quickly as I could in case something had happened.

"Hey man, how's it going?" I said.

Heavy breathing came through the phone—just like the breathing that came over the walkie-talkie.

"Hello? Dude, what's up?" I asked, a little concerned.

More heavy breathing, then the call dropped.

"What the—" I was confused, so I called his number back.

"Hey brother, what's up?" Marvin said as he answered the phone.

"Well, you tell me. What just happened?" I asked.

"I'm not sure what you mean," he said.

"I just got a call from you and there was just heavy breathing into the phone, just like the breathing we heard come over the walkies on that first night," I explained.

"I've had my phone right here with me. I haven't made any calls all day except when we talked earlier," he told me.

"Are you serious? Are you messing with me?" I persisted.

Marvin confirmed he had not made any calls, so we wrapped up our conversation.

There seemed to be one coincidence after another piling on top of each other. Physically I felt pretty well at the time, though there was a bit of psychological warfare beginning. I felt comforted by the fact that we had the full support of everyone down there, so it was easy to stay focused on the task at hand. Everyone involved felt like the story needed to be told, so I sat at my desk putting the details of the upcoming investigation together.

My phone rang very late. It was my brother.

"Hey buddy, what's up?" I greeted him.

"Well, I don't know what is going on, but something is crazy. Ever since you left, we have been seeing shadows all over the house. They just dart from room to room. Dad came by earlier too and you won't believe what happened when he was leaving," he said.

"What happened?" I asked.

"As he was leaving, I walked out front with him and suddenly a big ball of light came out of nowhere and bolted down just over our heads and seemed like it crashed into the house! It was insane! It was big, like bigger than a basketball. We both reacted and kind of ducked because it came out of nowhere. When I grabbed the door to go back in, it was like I got electrocuted," he said.

"Are you serious? It just came out of nowhere and then disappeared into the house?" I didn't know what to say.

"Yeah, Dad was flustered. I didn't know what to do or say. We went back into the house just to see if anything crazy had happened and we didn't find anything. But since that happened, Jenn and I have seen shadows a lot. We've seen them here before, but today there are a lot of them," he continued.

"Damn, I had some crazy shit going on here before I came over. That place is just different than any other place we've been. It just doesn't stop. Gerald has told me over and over again that things will follow us. Everyone needs to be really sure they want to participate in this project. I don't know what is going to happen next, and I have no idea how bad things might get," I said.

"Oh, we are going, buddy. I have to check this place out. We will burn some sage and see if that helps over here," he finished.

Snort didn't scare easily; he also didn't deny what was right in front of his face either. I had no doubt what he told me was true. At that point, I was simply happy that nobody was hurt.

We all knew we would have to be careful about cleansing our vehicles and ourselves before coming home following a trip down there.

The project was beginning to consume me; I felt it in my heart. If I was not reviewing the data we had collected at the location, I was thinking about the next time we would go down there. It was both exhilarating and torturous at the same time. If we could not collectively accept the potential consequences of our investigations, we knew it would be time to walk away. The draw of the potential enlightenment was too much for any of us to deny. Our work had become part of us long ago.

THIRTEEN

Team, Tahlequah; Tahlequah, Team

ON THAT NIGHT THE sky would be black with the pending new moon. Jason Buis, Jared, Jenn, Snort, and I made the trek from home into the abyss that was Tahlequah. The weather was perfect on that late spring day. The calm was eerie, and for the first time, I had noticed not a sound being made all around us. There was not even a light breeze. No birds. Nothing. A perfect stillness—and it was terrifying.

The property was abandoned when we arrived in the afternoon. Marvin was at work, Gerald had gone out of town for the weekend, and Annette was elsewhere making preparations for dinner, as she always did. When we came to see our friends, the hospitality was beyond anything I had ever experienced with clients. We were welcomed not only as friends, but as family. After I parked the car, we all got out and everyone began wandering the grounds. I stood outside the car and took some deep breaths in anticipation of what might lie ahead.

I knew I was at the behest of the land; it was a world of wonder, beauty, and horror all wrapped in one overwhelming package. I had to keep my faith strong in knowing we were all where we needed to be. In many ways I felt as though the demons of my past were held at bay while I was there. I had no idea if it was a good thing or a bad thing, but that was how it felt. There was a freedom that came with it, although I never allowed myself to forget the potential of trading one nightmare for another, so my guard needed to be up at all times.

When your feet slumped into the soft ground and your heart skipped a beat with the knowledge that something invisible was very likely watching your every move, imagination became a reality in the blink of an eye.

I reminded everyone to pay attention to everything, no matter where they were on the property. Jared had pointed out the old house to confirm it was where we were headed.

"Wow, okay. Is there a weight limit in there?" Jared said as we all laughed.

Jared had begun filming when we had arrived. We wanted to make sure we had some type of equipment running at all times. Jason and Jenn had walked toward Gerald's house. They had decided to spend time together because she had wanted to see if her sensitivities coincided with his thoughts and feelings. Jared, Snort, and I made our way to the house to get our equipment set up.

"You weren't kidding, buddy, the ground is soft. In spots it feels like quicksand!" Snort said.

"Yeah, at least Marvin chopped through most of the overgrowth. It was a lot worse when we had to chop through the brush," I was interrupted.

"WHOA!" Snort yelled.

I suddenly became paralyzed as a large branch came crashing to the ground without so much as a crack and slammed to the ground about five feet from where I stood. The widow-maker shook the ground as it landed; its circumference was larger than my arms could reach around, and it was almost ten feet in length. I stood, frozen, without words—I knew I was a couple steps from being worm food.

"Holy shit! Are you all right?!" Snort came rushing.

"Oh ... my ... God," Jared pointed the camera at me as he stood in shock.

"Um, yeah, it didn't land on me, so I suppose I'm just fine. What the hell just happened?" I replied, feeling stunned.

None of us had heard a thing. Normally there are many loud cracking sounds when a large branch breaks off a tree. It would presumably give any bystanders at least a couple seconds to make a move in one direction or another. Without a breeze in the air or a sound as it fell, the huge branch came violently out of nowhere and crashed into the ground with the force of a high-speed car crash. The three of us stood in silence, stunned, not knowing how to interpret what just happened. After taking a couple minutes to appreciate being alive, we continued moving toward the house.

As we approached the house, we turned on our Ovilus X *[OX]* device and began recording on multiple recorders. The Ovilus was not used to collect what we would typically refer to as evidence, but it could potentially provide relevant thoughts into the ongoing investigation.

The device spoke in what sounded like a robotic voice and is said to use fluctuations in the environment (such as electromagnetic energy changes, temperature changes, etc.) to formulate and speak words. The theory behind the technology suggested that intelligent spirits were sometimes able to manipulate certain aspects of the surrounding environment, allowing for words to be spoken from the device that could be relevant to the current situation. The hope was that the device would provide spoken words that might go along with potential EVPs we might capture during the question and answer sessions. We wanted to have as many pieces of equipment that could correlate the actions of one another as we could. If there were reactions from our EMF detectors, coupled with voices captured by our recorders, and potentially intelligent words being spoken by the Ovilus, it could make for a pretty compelling testimony that something "paranormal" could be occurring.

The three of us entered the house and I gave them the tour of the small, decrepit place.

"*CRASH; ACCIDENT.*" *[OX]*

"Dude, did you hear that? This freaking thing just said 'crash' and 'accident' back to back! Are you talking about the tree branch that just crashed to the ground outside?" I asked.

"You sure that was an accident?" Snort said.

BOOM!

We all jumped from a sudden sound that came from the Room of Faces. Since we had walked into the house, the pressure was building in my ears.

"What the hell?" Jared's back was to the room and he jumped when he heard the sound.

We all quickly headed into the Room of Faces.

"That door has been open ever since I started coming into this house—it leads to the back of the house. There are no floors on the other side," I informed them as I opened the door that led to the back of the house.

"Well, it isn't open now. Try slamming it shut and see if it's the same sound," my brother said.

BOOM—the sound was recreated as I slammed the door with force.

"Yeah, I'd say that is exactly what just happened," I said.

"DEATH." [OX]

"What death are you talking about?" I asked.

"Brandon, missed." [RT-EVP]

"I just heard my name," I said as I heard the playback after a couple seconds. "Are you welcoming us? There are some new people here, friends of mine, do you know their names?" I continued.

"Something just tapped me on the shoulder, like, blatantly," Snort said.

It had become clear with the sun still blazing upon the grounds that it could be a very interesting night. Jared was doing his best to keep a camera on both my brother and me as we continued to work our way through the house. We had run cable from Gerald's house to provide power to the house, so we were working on setting up some additional equipment.

Jared finished setting up our power supplies throughout the house as we got a couple more cameras set up and connected to our remote digital video recorder (DVR) system. This would allow us to visually monitor the house from a remote location. Marvin had mentioned he wanted to spend some time watching the cameras throughout the night. We also plugged in and powered on an EMF pump. Jason had made the pump; the idea behind it was to provide additional atmospheric energy to the area, so anything present that was looking for energy to manifest would have plenty at its disposal. On many occasions, investigators are wiped of their energy when in the presence of potential spirit activity. It gave us a way to provide plenty of energy to whatever might be hanging out in the house and hopefully give it a chance to show us what it could do when the atmosphere was supercharged. The levels of EMF throughout the property were nearly 0 milligauss (mG) at all times, with occasional fluctuations. At that point, all rooms in the house were reading a consistent and significantly higher reading because of the pump we had placed in the kitchen, the central location of the house. The kitchen was then reading at about 40–75 mG, a huge number.

The surrounding rooms were reading between 5 mG and 15 mG; the levels varied constantly, but we had confirmed there was constant energy throughout the house.

"So you've been chatty so far, we brought you something that might help you communicate with us better. You have said you need energy, well, here is all the energy you might need," I explained to whatever may have been listening.

"Can you please show us what you are capable of? I am just trying to document what you can do; we are giving you a constant energy source. Will that help you?" I continued.

"Energy, given." [EVP]

The sound of a piano began softly coming from the living room.

"Whoa! Shh. Do you guys hear that?" I said.

As I stepped into the living room from the kitchen, the sound of the piano stopped. I carefully crossed the living room and reached the piano to confirm that it was no longer functional. I slid my finger from one end of the keys to the other; it didn't make a sound other than a thud as the keys clunked down.

"Was the freaking thing just playing?" My brother asked as he joined me.

"Well, I have a few recorders running and I heard it clear as day through the RT-EVP, so I don't know where else the sound would have come from. But it doesn't work, I've tried it before," I told him.

After a few more minutes in the house, we completed our setup of cameras and equipment. We decided to head back to the driveway as Marvin had pulled up and greeted Jason and Jenn. The house was armed with equipment from many angles, so we had hopes of something making itself known that evening.

Footsteps slowly walked across the wooden floor with a distinct thump, followed by a faint laughing sound.

"Energy." [OX]

After the investigation that evening, we discovered there were many sounds going on inside the house. It seemed as though the energy pump was working very well.

We gathered back near the campfire and dinner table. Marvin showed me what was left of the three scratches that he had received. He also showed me three new scratches he had received more recently. He told me the feeling of being watched was constant.

I explained to him everything that had been going on since we arrived. It had been a very active afternoon and evening. Marvin told me he would like to join us during some of the investigations, so I was interested to see if anything responded differently with him present.

Gerald had also joined us as we all sat down around the fire and ate Annette's wonderful chili. There was a distinct feeling of camaraderie and closeness with the entire group as we sat around getting to know one another.

After Gerald and Marvin reiterated their interest in the project, they extended an open invitation to us all. I asked the brothers to join me in the house, so the three of us made our way in that direction.

"Are you in here? I brought Gerald and Marvin with me. Do you know them?" I asked.

"Did you scratch me?" Marvin immediately said. "Do you watch me?"

"Gerald, do you have any questions?" I asked him as he stood curiously in the corner of the room.

Laughing, "No, I think I will just see what happens," he told me.

"Buried." [OX]

"What is buried? Where?" I asked.

"Angry." [OX]

All three of us reacted to the strange words streaming from the Ovilus. I reiterated to Gerald and Marvin that whatever came from the box shouldn't be entirely trusted.

"Marvin, Gerald, go, now." [EVP]

We continued the line of questioning for several more minutes as the sun disappeared quickly in the background of the Room of Faces. The house went pitch-black in a matter of seconds.

"I'm heading back to the fire. This place is too spooky," Gerald said.

Marvin and I continued our line of questioning as he had felt the need to ask more questions.

"You okay?" I asked Marvin as he had grown distant and quiet.

"Yeah, you feel that?" He asked me.

"Right this second, I feel irritable," I told him.

"Exactly, something in here just makes people mad," he said.

A few more minutes passed and I decided it was time to head back to meet up with the crew. When Marvin and I got back to the fire, Gerald, Annette, and Jared were there. Jason, Jenn, and Snort had wandered off to check out a few different places on the property.

Gerald and Annette retired for the evening; Jared and I had talked to Marvin about going into the house at 3:00 a.m.

At about 2:45 a.m., we all headed up to the house to see what might happen between 3:00 and 4:00 a.m. We strategically placed ourselves around the house. Jenn and Snort stationed themselves in the living room, Jared and Jason in the back room, and myself and Marvin in the kitchen and Room of Faces.

We all sat quietly for several minutes. The house was still.

"Ah!" Jenn jumped.

"What the—" Snort hesitated.

"Something just grabbed my legs!" Jenn said.

"Same here, what the hell," Snort confirmed.

At that precise moment, I lost track of what I was thinking; I remember seeing red. Outside of feeling my blood pressure skyrocket, I had to rely on the cameras and audio rolling at the time to remember exactly what happened.

"What's the matter?" Marvin asked me.

"*Death.*" *[OX]*

"*Come to us.*" *[EVP]*

I walked by Marvin on my way into the Room of Faces. "You messing with me?" I yelled as I slammed my foot into the wall as hard as I could, leaving a hole in the wall.

"Did you just hear that?" Jared said to Jason from the back room.

Jason jumped as my foot slammed into the wall. "Laughing?" He said to Jared.

"Yeah dude, clear as day, right between us," he said as he made his way to the doorway.

"What the hell!" Snort said as he and Jenn made their way into the kitchen. "You okay, buddy?" He asked in my direction.

"Goddamn, my foot hurts," I said as I was making my way to the kitchen.

"It's hot in here, I'm dizzy, I need to get outside," I said as I lowered my head and made my way to the door.

"What just happened?" Jared whispered rhetorically to Jason.

"He just snapped, that was spooky," Marvin said. Everyone followed me out of the house.

The crew made their way back to the burning embers of the fire that had once been a huge blaze. The dizziness had given way to clarity. Everyone pulled up a chair and Marvin brought some more wood over and stoked the flames.

"Let's tear down soon, it's time to go," I said.

Everyone sat down and almost an hour passed before a word was said. Everyone had been wiped of all energy. We would have to review everything collected to put the entire story together. Everyone had had enough for the evening.

I told Marvin I would be in touch and we all said our goodbyes. The drive home seemed like an eternity. Everyone was completely exhausted; hardly a word was spoken. Everybody took turns dozing, and eventually we all made our way to our own beds. It had been a very memorable night for many reasons. So much had happened; we had asked the land and the energy that inhabits it to show us what it could do. Everybody had their own experiences that evening, and none of us would forget any of it. The investigation would be known as a success; it would also be remembered as one of the most terrifying nights we had ever experienced.

It had taken very little time for Oklahoma to get inside me. It felt as though there was a tug of war going on between the powerful, ageless forces I was surrounded by and those of my past. I was standing in a beautiful world of horror, and I was at its mercy. It was not just a house or a plot of land; it was a way of life that went back more years than I could count. In many ways, I felt as though the demons of the past were held at bay while I was there. I didn't know if that was a good thing or a bad thing. I had no doubt in my mind that whatever was stalking me in Oklahoma was very formidable. I did not know what might happen in the days to come, but

I knew I had the attention of whatever was down there. All I could do was continue my quest and hope that it would not escalate to a dangerous level—assuming it hadn't already.

FOURTEEN

Side Effects

I QUICKLY AWOKE AND was shaking like a leaf in a stiff breeze. My breathing was approaching hyperventilating levels as I lay on my back, knowing that something wasn't right. As I attempted to sit up, my bent knee thumped against something hard. I felt panic setting in from head to toe as my forehead thumped against something solid. Suddenly I realized I couldn't move—I couldn't get up. My breathing continued to escalate. I could hear muffled voices at a distance; I could hear the beating of drums.

I began to scramble but could not move in any direction. I heard the thunderous storm of something being piled on top of me, just inches away. I felt claustrophobic as I wiggled my hands to my chest and began thumping on the wood just above my body. I felt around in all directions and began kicking with my feet; I was surrounded. Another thunderous roar came crashing down around me. I could feel the weight of it pressing down on the frame that surrounded me. This couldn't be happening. How did I get here? More rumbling came crashing down above me. I couldn't escape; I had no strength and very little breath. The beating of the drum became more and more faint following each crash. The voices were only whispers. I was being buried alive.

I was able to maneuver a lighter from my pocket and bring it to my chest; I clicked it several times before it ignited. As I had feared, I was surrounded by dust and wood that gave way to just a few inches on every side of me. A mumbled grumbling came down on top of me as the dirt leaked through the small cracks of the box and fell upon my face. The lighter was getting weaker by the second; I could feel the air being suffocated from the enclosure. I knew I might have just minutes to live; every breath was becoming more and more of a struggle. My mind felt broken as I began to yell. The sound of my voice could not travel through my surroundings—surely nobody could hear me. I began to scratch and claw at the wood, splinters puncturing my skin as the pain shot through me like a knife. This was the end.

The lighter went out as I lay in pitch blackness. The thundering sounds I had been hearing were now muted; the drumbeats were gone. I felt myself snap and give in to my grave; I only hoped the pain would not linger. Breathing was scarcely an option now, as my lungs felt like overinflated balloons ready to pop at any second. As I lay still, accepting my fate, a lone tear streamed from my eye. My waning thoughts were of my children, my family, and my friends. I never meant for things to end this way.

"Help me."

A child's voice rang out as I came to. My breathing was heavy and I was covered in cold sweat as I shot upright in my bed. I could feel the tears roll down my face. I felt like I had just met my demise being suffocated under the ground. I had been awakened from the nightmare by the sound of a child I had heard so clearly several times before.

Sleep had become a thing of the past; one restless night after another left my mind and body feeling exhaustion's wrath. It had become more difficult to function in everyday life as mundane functions became chores; every ounce of energy was zapped for days upon my return from Oklahoma.

It was early in the morning; the sun had not begun to crack the horizon, so I decided to go for a walk hoping to calm my mind and nerves. There was an old cemetery that I frequented that was about a half-mile away from the house. On that night the illumination of the few streetlights seemed oddly dim—there was a strange calm to the air. The house was located on the outskirts of the city, so it was common for the nighttime to wrap the entire area in a stranglehold as the countless stars provided the majority of the light. A subtle fog had rolled into the neighborhood. There was an ominous feeling in the air. The night was black and there was limited visibility.

I continued the short trek toward the cemetery as the feeling of being watched covered me like a blanket. I had been on edge because of the nightmare, and the level of exhaustion within me had peaked. The environment felt like a great opportunity to take some pictures. There was eeriness in the air with the combination of the fog and blackness of the night. Capturing the environment with pictures was very therapeutic.

I had been wandering aimlessly in the night for almost an hour; there was a hint of the impending sunrise over the horizon. The familiar glow began to pierce the darkness. There was a rustling within the confines of the cemetery; the leaves were being shuffled. I entered the cemetery with the intention of finding out what was causing the ruckus.

I approached the darkest remaining corner of the cemetery when the rustling came to a pause, and then a low grumbling sound came ahead of me. The grumbling became a growl as I snapped pictures into the darkness. As I swung around, I could see a large outline of a dog in the shadows. It was blacker than the darkness; its eyes had a dim, red glow. I stood about twenty feet from the animal and began to wonder why I did not sense any danger. I wondered if utter exhaustion had completely stolen the last bit of "give a damn" I had. The growl continued, I raised my camera in the direction of the beast, and I snapped three pictures; the flash was immediately followed by loud shuffling of leaves. The dog had disappeared into the darkness without a trace. I looked at the pictures I had taken, and there was no sign of the animal in any of them. I began to wonder if I had officially lost my mind. The sun began to creep into sight; the darkness gave way to the fall's morning glow. I headed back home hoping to get some rest. I was perplexed by what had just happened. I did not feel in danger, and I wondered if everything had been a figment of my imagination or if I had been stalked by the largest dog I had ever seen.

Gerald had been right; Tahlequah had made its way into my soul, and it took very little time to do so. The land was the most paranormally active place I had ever been. The lore, the lust, the mind-bending reality was almost beyond comprehension. It was terrifying and addictive, beautiful and horrific at the same time.

"It will follow you," Gerald's prophetic words rang in my mind.

I had no idea what was following me. I knew there were depths to this project that we had never touched before; part of me continuously remembered mistakes made in the past. I feared the potential of something similar happening in the future. The project meant a lot to everybody involved, but I had to ask myself if we had found ourselves treading in waters that could end up drowning us all.

I believed there was a reason we were led to the land that had been soaked in both blood and tears of the true forefathers and mothers of the land. Our immediate connection with our friends in Oklahoma, coupled with all the strange occurrences all around us, seemed to confirm we had uncovered something very unique.

"Humanity weeps over the fate of the Indians, but true philanthropy reconciles the mind to the extinction of one generation for another," Andrew Jackson is quoted as saying. Jackson had made it clear that his conscience was at ease following his attempted genocide of a people that had inhabited the land for hundreds, if not thousands, of years. The land had been invaded by murderers intent on building a new world on the back of greed, torture, and malevolence toward anybody with physical or spiritual differences.

At that point, the pieces felt like they were beginning to fall into place. There had been a secrecy that we were greeted with; it took months to build up a certain level of trust with our new friends. These peaceful, spiritual people had been invaded and subsequently massacred and robbed as pure evil took hold of the land they called home. The land had been their protector and provider for generations. The white man had come and brought with them nightmares and devastation. In the years that followed the devastation, the Native people were swept under a rug and segregated after being given small plots of land and reservations. Walls built up so thick and high made it impossible for a small group of people to break them down.

We felt honored to have been graced with such friendships and the chance to explore their land. We were lucky to share their stories and heritage as we experienced the palpable energy of the region.

FIFTEEN

Flying Solo

I WAS EXPERIENCING NIGHTMARES and strange occurrences almost every day. Marvin let me know he had again been scratched and awakened at 3:33 a.m. several times that week; we decided we should get together the coming weekend.

Nobody else was able to make the trip that weekend, so I was left with a decision. I normally did not make it a practice to investigate alone, and I was not too thrilled about the idea of going down there on my own. There is a very real danger in investigating alone, but I felt I had to get down there and spend some time with my friends. At that point, they felt like my second family. I packed my bags that morning and hit the road and headed south on US-69 and looked forward, albeit with a certain level of trepidation, to another potentially eventful evening. I had no idea how involved Marvin or anybody else would be that night; however, I felt like I needed to have my own experiences. I needed the solitude that came with being alone.

As I pulled into the driveway, Marvin and Annette were there to greet me with open arms. The yard area in front of the abandoned shack had been freshly cleared, the huge yard within the circle drive had been cut, and the bonfire area was all set up for the night. Gerald joined us shortly after I arrived; he seemed jovial on that particular evening.

Annette had continued our tradition of having dinner as a group. Prior to each investigation, we made a point to break bread with one another and share our lives, laughs, and stories with each other.

"Things have been crazy around here," Gerald said, "those knocking sounds, the yelling in the woods, just crazy. I don't go out when y'all aren't here after dark, no way!" He said laughing. Gerald would often tell us terrifying stories but would almost always end by somehow making himself and whomever he was speaking to laugh. It was his way of bringing levity to any situation; he always wanted to look at things from a very spiritual and educational perspective.

"Yeah, you can still see the scratches on my chest," Marvin said as he exposed the higher side of his chest under his shirt. He didn't seem too distraught about the scratches; he just seemed to want to be more and more involved as unexplainable things happened.

Marvin showed me some pictures he had taken of the deep scratches shortly after it had happened.

"I worry about you boys," Annette said. "Sometimes I can feel that energy and it is so scary," she finished.

Annette did not involve herself in the investigations very often. She always had a plate of hot food and a cooler full of water and soda ready for however many people we ended up bringing to the land. Soon after, we all filled our bellies and shared some laughs as the perfect summer day carried on.

Gerald informed us that he would be heading into town for the evening. I decided to go ahead and get my equipment organized and prepared to set up. I packed up a couple video cameras, their tripods, and some additional gadgets. I headed over the soft ground toward the house. There was not much daylight left, so I needed to hustle to get everything set up before the sun took its leave behind the hills.

I could feel the eyes on me from every direction as I approached the house; a level of discomfort was never far away when it came to the surroundings of the house. I made my way through the scorched entrance at the side of the house. As I made my way down the short, narrow hallway, I made a right turn into the kitchen area. I knew where I wanted to set up the equipment in order to give me good visual coverage of the place. I headed directly across the kitchen and into the Room of Faces. The pressure in my ears began to build as I walked into the room. I noticed the largest couple of wasps I had ever seen in my life. There were small nests peeking through different places throughout the house. I had no doubt that the size of the nests was simply an illusion, hiding what was surely a much larger nest in the space above the ceilings. Being allergic to them, I did my best to make my way through the rooms without drawing much attention from the winged creatures.

I set up my tripod and a digital camcorder in the Room of Faces so it was looking into the kitchen area from the back corner of the room. It allowed me to keep the mirror and the side door within view, and it gave me a good look into the kitchen as well. I set up the camera and pressed record. "Here is one of the cameras, make sure you say hello at some point tonight, it's just us tonight," I said as I made my way back into the kitchen to set up the other camera.

"Brandon, hey," [RT-EVP] a raspy voice whispered in my ear.

Chills ran up my spine as I heard the all too familiar voice.

"Yeah, here I am. I am all alone tonight; do you have plans?" I responded, attempting to get real-time communication going.

I got no further response for a minute or two, so I continued to set up the tripod in the kitchen. There was a deafening silence that surrounded me in that decrepit place; the silence was even more eerie than the typical sounds of nature that often surrounded us. Everything was still—too still.

As I placed the camera on the tripod, the room suddenly felt dark; the waning sunlight no longer had any effect on the bowels of the shack. I had aimed the camera into the living room from the kitchen so it would cover most of both rooms and give good coverage of the majority of the house in case anything decided to make its presence known.

Laughing sound. [RT-EVP]

I felt a blanket of dread thrown over my entire body as I heard the menacing laugh in my ear. Suddenly I was overcome with anxiety and fear. The entire house had taken a turn, and it felt like something bad was about to happen.

"Seriously? I can't even set up my equipment?" I said in frustration.

"*BEWARE*" *[OX]*, the robotic voice rang clear from across the room. The feeling of danger grew by the second as I sped up to complete my equipment setup.

"*ALONE.*" *[OX]*

"Yeah, I am alone, is that going to be okay with you?" I responded as I saw the readout of the word on the Ovilus.

"*Go!*" *[RT-EVP]*

"I just got here, I can't go yet," I responded as I heard the same voice in my ear.

At that point, I felt like I needed to get out of the house; it was overwhelming. I had felt panic set in countless times during investigations in the past. Being in total solitude and surrounded by total darkness, I had a difficult time maintaining my composure. I had a recorder and two cameras running, along with the Ovilus and an EMF detector that would alarm with large fluctuations of electromagnetic energy. I felt like I had a sufficient amount of data being collected, so I began to make my way into the narrow hallway so I could head outside to catch my breath.

A growling sound came from the back room as I walked down the hallway.

I naturally sped up down the hall and left the house behind me. I was attempting to ignore the fact that the black dog I had recently made acquaintances with might very well be right behind me, ready to devour me at any moment. Right then I couldn't get out of the house fast enough.

When I broke through the doorway and made my way into the yard area, I looked behind me and could swear I saw red, glowing eyes at the end of the dark hallway. It was clear the night would be a true test. I had never spent much time investigating on my own, but I knew Marvin would be present for at least part of the evening. I also felt it important to attempt to connect to the place on a personal level. The house seemed to indicate its willingness to participate, given the time I had already spent in there before the sun went down. Only time would tell as to what might happen, but it was clear that something would happen. I made my way back to the bonfire area, my senses on high alert. There were eyes on me from every direction. The feeling was unsettling, but it was no longer foreign.

"You doin' all right?" Marvin asked as I sat down.

"Yeah, something is up, that's for sure. Could be a long night," I confirmed. "Where did Annette run off to?"

"Oh, she had to go into the office, so she took off," he told me.

"Looks like it's just me and you then," I said, staring off into the distance toward the setting sun as Marvin nodded.

"I have to pull the late shift tonight, so I will need to leave here around ten or so. You can stay as long as you'd like. Gerald may not be home until tomorrow though, so it would just be you. Just be careful out here," Marvin told me. His words sent shivers up my spine.

"Cool. I may not pull an all-nighter, but I will probably hang out for a little while. I think most of it will depend on what is going on," I confirmed.

Marvin and I made our way into the house as the darkness dug in its heels for the night. I had let him know about the feelings I had when I was inside setting up the equipment.

"That dog, I feel like I've seen that dog around here too. It's a big ol' black dog and it just comes and goes. The old folks might tell you it's an omen and could mean bad things are gonna happen," he told me.

"Yeah, I have heard of things like this in different cultures, but never in Native American culture though. It seems like you all have endless symbols for almost every animal; I have never seen or heard anything like it before. I've heard growling before, but this was chilling. I actually thought I was about to get mauled," I said.

"I have never felt like it approached me, but I seen it plenty of times. There are a lot of dogs out there, but this one is twice the size of any of them, black as night, and its eyes glow blood red. Creepy stuff," Marvin said.

"That is pretty much exactly what I have seen and heard."

As we entered the house, Marvin was immediately drawn to the back room, so we took a left from the narrow hallway and entered the room as the floor sunk beneath our feet. We both found a cross board to stand on so we had some better footing. The ceiling seemed as though it would fall on top of us at any time. Pieces of the ceiling had eroded away so badly they were like dirty icicles hanging over our heads. As soon as we settled into the room, the K-II meter in my hand began lighting up. There were five lights on it; the more that illuminated, the stronger the signal that was being detected. The first three lights were immediately on and were holding strong. I had a recorder in my hand.

"*CLOSET*" *[OX]*, the Ovilus spoke clearly from its stand in the kitchen. Marvin immediately made his way around the junk pile in the room toward the closet in the corner as the fourth and fifth lights perked up on the K-II meter.

"You want me to find something in this closet?" Marvin asked. The five lights remained steadily lit on the meter.

"Dude, are you seeing this? The EMF around the whole property has been flat the entire time we've been here. This is crazy. This thing almost never lights up all five lights," I pointed out to Marvin as he approached the closet.

"What am I supposed to find in all this junk?" he said.

"Can you please turn the lights off on the meter so we can tell what you need us to find? I can ask you questions and you can respond with lighting them up. Can you do that please?" I asked as the lights went out.

"Wow," Marvin said.

"Okay, thank you. Can you please light up two lights for the answer YES and three lights for the answer NO?" I asked as two lights were lit.

"So to confirm, two lights means YES, right?" I said, looking for further validation as the first two lights on the device blinked several times.

The lights were out on the device as I told Marvin to proceed with his questions.

"Are you kin?" he asked. Two lights came on.

"Daddy?" The lights went out.

"Is that you, Mom?" he asked as two lights lit up.

"Damn, dude," I said. "Okay, thank you very much. Can you please turn the lights off so Marvin can ask you another question?" The lights went out.

"Mom, you want me to find something in this closet?" Marvin asked as the lights came on.

"JACKET" [OX] came from the kitchen in a robotic voice.

"Dude, do you see a jacket in there?" I was flabbergasted. "Be careful, man, this is the first time we have had any indicator at all that someone in your family was trying to communicate."

"Are you just messin' with me, or is this really you?" Marvin continued as he reached into the closet and pulled out a jacket that was on a hanger.

All five lights came on strong and held just as soon as our line of questioning turned skeptical.

"Okay, turn them off please. Is Marvin holding the right jacket?" I asked as all the lights went out for a few seconds and then came back on strong.

Marvin proceeded to dig through the pockets of his father's old military jacket that had been hanging in the closet and he pulled out a picture. We both looked at one another.

"Is this what you wanted me to find?" Marvin asked as the meter fell to two solid lights.

"What is it a picture of? This is incredible," I asked as Marvin handed it to me. It was a picture of his mother and father from a very long time ago.

"*DANGER*" [OX] chimed in from the kitchen.

"Are you telling us we are in danger, Momma?" Marvin asked as the two lights on the meter went out and quickly came back on strong.

"Are we safe here?" I asked as the third light came on. "No, we are not safe, is that right?" The meter dropped to two lights.

After holding strong for a few more seconds, it was as if nothing had ever happened. For the next several minutes, our line of questioning could not convince the lights to budge. It was as though nothing had ever happened.

Marvin and I spent the next hour in the house with varying degrees of interaction. When he would hold the K-II meter, it seemed to trigger more interaction. None of the interactions were as lengthy or seemingly intelligent as the first. There were moments when we both felt very uncomfortable in each room; there were also times that neither of us felt anything around us at all. The Ovilus continued to spit out words on occasion, but it was difficult to make sense of most of them. I had been wearing the RT-EVP almost the entire time, but had not heard anything out of the ordinary. The time was drawing near to when Marvin would have to head to work, so we decided to head back to the campfire to take a little break before he packed up for the evening. Before we left the house, I could feel the pressure building in my ears. I was beginning to feel nervous about the idea of being in there alone.

"Momma, you still here? I have to go soon. Momma, you here?" Marvin asked as we slowly began making our way toward the hallway. The light on the K-II meter illuminated as strongly as it could as soon as he finished his question.

"Look," I told Marvin as he looked down to the light glowing in his hand.

"I love ya, Momma. We miss you," Marvin said as all the lights on the meter lit up.

Marvin and I headed down the hallway and out the door; we strolled silently through the yard area and made our way to the glowing fire that had fallen to nothing more than a sweltering heat source. As we got back to the fire, we put a few logs on and it quickly lit back up and began to reach for the sky.

"Do you really think that was my mom?" Marvin asked.

"I honestly don't know, man. It's nearly impossible to say. All I know is after almost every interaction we have had throughout the entire time, I haven't had any indication at all that your family members may be in there," I told him. "That isn't to say it isn't possible. For all I know, all the energy around here can go wherever it wants, whenever it wants. Maybe it is her and she saw you come inside with me, so she came along," I continued as the lights on the K-II meter came on strong as if to say YES.

"The one thing I need to be clear on though—make sure you don't buy in totally. Whatever is here that I have run into is really smart and crafty; what better way to get close to you than to make you think it's your mom?" I told Marvin as he nodded.

We paused, looked at each other, and knew without saying anything that either something was messing with our minds or it was very possible Gerald and Marvin's mother might be around, and might be looking over all of us. The light on the meter went out and did not come back on despite some attempts from both of us.

"I've never seen anything like that before," Marvin told me.

"Honestly, I've had some pretty cool interactions before, but I have never been led to something and spent ten full minutes getting immediate responses from yes or no questions. That was incredible," I told him.

We sat for a few more minutes as Marvin told me a little more about his parents while holding the picture he found. We both took turns looking at the photo; it was in remarkably good shape, considering the fact that it had spent so much time in such rough circumstances inside a rotting house. It was one of the most fascinating things I had seen in a long time, if not ever. I hoped that even though I hadn't heard any voices through the RT-EVP that I would find something in the review. I had several audio devices running throughout that session, but nothing came up that was distinct enough to label as audio communication.

As Marvin and I began to wind down our discussions, he began packing up his truck so he could head to work. In the distance we both heard a low grumbling sound.

"Looks like it might storm," Marvin said as the wind picked up noticeably, from dead calm to a steady breeze.

"Great, I'll keep my eyes out. Be careful while you're out, bro. I'll see you soon," I told him.

"You be careful too. The trailer is open if you need to head down there," Marvin gestured to his trailer down the driveway.

"Thanks. Talk to you soon," I said. He shut the truck door and drove away. The taillights grew dimmer as he made his way down the dirt road. Another grumble came from the distance as I stood alone.

SIXTEEN

A Dark and Stormy Night

Get your ass in gear. Time to go." My mind would not allow me to ignore what was heading my way.

I stood alone next to the fire as I stoked it with a few more logs. My mind and body seemed to be procrastinating—I felt like I could not take a step toward the house. My eyes were fixated on the distant flashes that lit up the sky, followed by the low grumbling of the thunder as it rolled directly toward me.

After a few minutes, I headed back toward the house. There was not a fiber in me that even wondered if the storm might work its way through the grounds; it was coming. The wind had picked up to a steady howl, so I left the peering eyes of the woods behind me as I walked into the house.

"I already have the equipment running; if the storm gets too bad, I won't be able to carry everything to the car because it will get soaked. Well, screw it, I guess it is what it is," I attempted to justify my presence. I knew I was quickly running out of time to change my mind as there was no way in hell I was prepared to transport all the equipment all the way down the driveway to where I had parked the car. At that point, I could only hope the storm would pass quickly and not present a problem.

"WARNING." [OX]
"BURIED." [OX]
"DANGER." [OX]

The Ovilus had perked up with one word after the other just as I stepped into the kitchen. The words were intimidating to say the least. The thunder grew nearer. I had only minutes before I would be engulfed in the storm. I felt more nervous with each clap of thunder, and I could see the flashing lightning as it became more threatening with each passing second.

"Oh hell," I thought to myself.

It seemed as though I was seeing shadow movement all around me; everywhere I looked, it was as though something was tormenting me, playing games with me. The rain came down in sheets in the blink of an eye and was accompanied by a loud boom of thunder and flash of lightning that broke the darkness. Out of the corner of my eye I thought I saw red eyes in the living room as I stood in the kitchen. I was completely trapped; the death grip of nature had taken hold of the land and I had nowhere to go.

All the EMF detectors lit up simultaneously and I swore I could hear cackling coming from outside the house. It was audible, even with the overwhelming sound of rain thrashing the damaged roof and the booming thunder. The laugh was maniacal. It was distinct, but it was impossible to distinguish between the natural chaos going on outside and anything that might be paranormal. I was without words, my line of questioning came to a halt; I couldn't say if it was because I was no longer interested in the response or if the berating I was giving myself for my ridiculous decision had finally taken precedence.

With every gust of wind I could feel a shift in the entire house; it was as though I had put myself in a suicidal situation. If the shanty came crashing down, as it felt like it could at any moment, there was nobody within miles that could offer any assistance. The service on my cell phone was shoddy at best. As the mayhem continued outside, it seemed to be matched by the furious energy within the walls of the house. I could feel every negative emotion I had ever felt boil to the surface at the same time. I didn't know if my mind or the ceiling would crack first, but it felt inevitable that something had to give.

Just a couple hours had passed; wondrous weather had been overcome by commotion in all directions. I had no idea if the storm was supposed to last or if it would pass quickly. I checked the weather application on my phone, which indicated the bulk of it would shortly be over me. I could suddenly feel myself surrounded by wickedness. The wind continued to howl, and the walls continued to creak as if threatening to give way at any moment. I knew to stay confined within those walls was pure insanity. I could leave all the equipment behind, hoping the house didn't swallow it permanently, and make a break for my car, or I could stick it out inside with the hope that the house could withstand one more brutal attack on top of the countless storms it had faced in the past. The storm bore down like a never-ending freight train. I stood in the kitchen and kept noticing the EMF detectors going off every few seconds. The Ovilus continued to provide words on occasion, but very few actually sunk in as my mind was fixed on getting the hell out of there the minute it felt safe.

With a crack of thunder and flash of lightning, my attention was directed toward the light in the Room of Faces. Three eroded, seemingly melted faces of pure evil stared through the windows with the storm at their backs. They all smiled with their mouths dropped open; I could hear the distinct cackling again and I could see the faces it birthed from. I could see their black eyes and blood-stained teeth. Their droopy faces were like a three-headed monster standing outside and enjoying the show inside the house. Within that split second, time seemed to stand still for an eternity. I felt sick to my stomach seeing what I had so clearly seen. Another bolt shot down; the light was almost blinding and the faces were gone. The drops of rain continued to pound the glass—there were no reflections, no images, nothing. At that moment, I felt like my heart would explode from my chest. The faces were gone, but were they going to come inside? There was absolutely nothing that would keep them at bay if they wanted to attack me with whatever physical powers they possessed. I stammered away from the Room of Faces and stepped backward into the kitchen as I tripped over the tripod that stood behind me. I caught myself on the counter that stood against the opposite wall and saved myself from face-planting into the ground. As I tried to get my composure, the front door swung open with a huge gust of wind and slammed against the wall.

"Son of a bitch" was all I could muster in my mind, but it surely sounded like murmuring coming out of my mouth. Needing to get out of the house was an understatement, but what awaited outside the walls terrified me as much as anything inside at that point. I was screwed. I had never felt panic of that magnitude; I thought I knew what true panic was, but this was different. My mind was being snapped like a twig. I was convinced I would not make it home alive and began to quietly pray for some type of comfort. I knew if I ever needed protection from a higher power, it was in that moment.

My mind repeated my options; the fetal position on a cold, damp floor seemed like a top contender at the moment. I could run, but run where? If I made it to my car, I felt like something would be there waiting. If I stayed where I was, something might consume what was left of my sanity and dine on my soul as an eternal dessert. The lightning continued to crash with greater frequency. The anticipation of seeing whatever the light might provide was the biggest psychological hurdle I faced at that point. I was more afraid of what might be revealed than I ever had been. The fact that I was suddenly the star of a very clichéd horror movie did not escape me. It was pathetic; the problem was that nobody was there to yell "cut" at the end of the scene. Nobody had died yet, so maybe the scene wasn't quite over.

"DEMON." [OX]

"Really?" I said to myself. I found myself incapable of being surprised at that moment when such a frightening word presented itself.

"I told you," [RT-EVP] a voice whispered.

I could not make out the words immediately, but I knew something had just addressed me after hearing the word "you." I was the only living person in the house, yet voices could still be heard as clearly as if someone was standing right next to me.

After a few more minutes, I could hear the wind and rain lightening up a bit. I would make my break for it at the first opportunity I was presented with, so I began to gather up the equipment. I brought the camera in from the Room of Faces and put it next to the second camera. I kept them pointing in opposite directions so I could at least record as much as possible in case something else happened. At that point in time, I figured the floor might open up and an army of zombies might crawl out of the ground and eat me, so there was no way I would stop recording.

After about twenty more minutes of trepidation, the storm passed with one last rattle of the house. As quickly as it blitzed through, the real-life nightmare seemed to be coming to an end. As it moved east to claim its next victim, the tempest left but an occasional grumble in its wake. The place had just torn me to shreds emotionally and physically. I began collecting my equipment and headed to the car. I did not move with any hustle, no haste whatsoever, but lazily and with my head slumped down. I was a shell of myself as I meandered through the darkness without the wherewithal or energy to care what might happen next.

Eventually, I treaded my way down the gravel driveway and through the sporadic puddles of water and Oklahoma mud. As I approached my car, I got within about ten feet when I violently vomited without warning on the side of the driveway. I crumbled to my knees, only hoping to tell the story. I was sure I was a dead man. After a few minutes of losing every last drop of fluid in my body, I managed to get back to my feet and stumble the remaining few feet to my car, throwing my lifeless body into the vehicle.

With the few ounces of energy I had left, I reached for a bottle of water and a cigarette. I lit it and sucked every last bit of nicotine I could from it as it sparked and burned like the embers of the bonfire just a few hours before. I was trembling to the bone as I drank the water like it was the first I had for days. The idea of driving almost five hours to get home was impossible, so I decided I would just rest my head and eyes right where I was. There was at least a resemblance of safety in my mind since I was in what was always a safe place to me, my car. The only good thing to come out of the most absurd situation I had ever voluntarily put myself into was in that moment, I no longer cared whether or not I was truly out of harm's way.

My eyes opened at the sound of a text message I had received on my phone: Marvin—*You ok, dude? Got pretty nasty there for a bit.*

I noted the time; it was almost 4:00 a.m. *Yeah, it's all good, thanks bro,* I replied as I turned the key to the ignition and started the car. A dense fog had rolled in; I caught a little bit of sleep and was ready to put Oklahoma in my rearview mirror for the night. I cut through the fog and made my way down the dirt road, happy to be doing it in one piece.

"Holy shit, you dumb son of a bitch, what the hell was that?" I mumbled to myself. I was not sure if I would ever tell another soul about the events of that night. It felt like something that was meant for me and only me. It was personal.

SEVENTEEN

The Geographical Connection

FOLLOWING THE EVENTS THAT had taken place during the last investigation, it seemed to take days to get any sort of exuberance back in my body. I had dived fully clothed and head first into the frigid water. When I emerged, there was no towel in sight. No gentle breeze or warm sunlight to help dry me off. I felt chilled to my bones for several days; the energy seemed to take longer and longer to wear off with each passing trip.

After spending a few days recovering from my solitary trip to Oklahoma, I sat down and found that the data I had collected proved useful. Some of the events that had taken place were beyond explanation and logic. I wouldn't have believed what I had lived through unless I could go back and relive the entire thing. Once I finished going through everything that had been documented, I decided to dig a little deeper into the theory that drove us to the general location in the first place. I had been fascinated with the notion that the earth provides specific locations that have more natural energy within them. To me, it seemed like a road map to finding not only significant historical stories to pursue but potential ways to anticipate paranormal activity. If the locations could be pinpointed on a map, I felt that I could learn exactly where I should be looking for cases to pursue. I had reason to believe there was at least some validity to the theory, as it had produced without fail to that point.

There were historical ties to ley lines going back as far as man. Many people believe there is a direct connection with Stonehenge and ley lines; there are also ties from the great pyramids of Egypt to ley lines. The question was how did ancient civilizations learn that these lines existed, let alone where their exact locations were? I had to work with a software program that allowed me to get in the proverbial ballpark as far as where these lines were located. I decided to concentrate my efforts in the locations and surrounding areas of the places where these lines intersect. This gave me a greater chance to find myself on or very close to the actual location. I did develop an archive of all intersecting line locations in each state throughout the United States; this gave me the ability to look more closely at these locations and the surrounding communities. I attempted to narrow down each intersecting line to notable towns and cities within a fairly short distance of the alleged intersecting lines, typically within a maximum of a fifty-mile radius. While that seemed like a really large area, understanding these maps were not exact, I wanted to leave some room for error. A fifty-mile area is actually not very big when discussing the vastness of an entire state or even country. I felt that would allow me to narrow the search a little and focus on areas that were as close as possible to the intersections.

Throughout the continental United States, a number of areas have multiple intersecting ley lines at one particular location. For example, when viewing the map of Tahlequah, Oklahoma, there are four different lines that intersect right over the top of the town. In my hometown of Kansas City, there are two lines intersecting—these are just examples. There are also locations that have nine lines intersecting at one location. One example of this type of intersection is right in the heart of the infamous Bermuda Triangle. As the lines are drawn, they stretch out just as latitude and longitude lines appear on the map; however, these lines go in all different directions. Algeria is the home to one of the largest clusters of intersecting lines in the world. This is notable because in recent years Algeria has been notorious for a lot of strange occurrences. Mass deaths of animals, natural disasters, and many other things seem to be more prevalent in and around these locations.

As I dug deeper into the northeast Oklahoma region, specifically the area closely surrounding Tahlequah, I found more and more reports of unidentified flying objects, Sasquatch, and all sorts of strange sightings or encounters with creatures usually only spoken of in fairy tales and horror movies. I found it more and more difficult to ignore the many "coincidences" that came with the work we were doing in Tahlequah. Some people would say these large areas of intersecting lines were gateways to hell or a vortex to other dimensions. This is such a profound idea that most people find it much easier to simply dismiss these things as conspiracy theories or overactive imaginations. Those skeptics may be right, but if there is an objective look taken from all angles, the many stories, claims, and documented occurrences would force anybody to at least entertain the idea that there could be something significant to this.

What I felt I had on my hands was a very old, very powerful, and incredibly active location that might have its own agenda. It could have been as simple as whatever energy lingered simply wanted living people to leave it alone. I didn't believe that to be the case because I had really begun to feel like this energy needed to have other energy to feed on, so if there were no people there, how would it feed? Knowing it was likely that the geographical and historic significance were somehow linked was the intimidating part.

Further research into the locations of some well-known Indian burial mounds throughout the United States also showed the tendency for these sacred lands to be on or in very close proximity to ley lines. It was as if the old world knew these lines as though they were some type of spiritual highway. One does not have to dig too deep now to find a significant location just about anywhere, not only in the United States but throughout the entire world, so we had to be careful about making any assumptions. At that time, we were simply collecting data and hoping our research would lead us to some solid answers.

I decided to lay the map of the Trail of Tears over the map of ley lines. I was completely floored as I stared at it. I was unable to find words to show either complete terror or elation at the fact that I might have uncovered another piece of a seemingly endless puzzle. The Trail of Tears was broken into several different routes and paths; however, they all closely followed the flow of intersecting ley lines from start to finish. Outside of the Allen family, the Trail of Tears and ley lines had been my two main research points and they just had a head-on collision before my very eyes.

The routes taken followed lines running east and west, sometimes meandering to the north and south, but the two locations that stood out the most were the middle and end points of the Trail of Tears. Hopkinsville, Kentucky, was within fifty miles of four lines intersecting right near Bowling Green, one of the main paths of the Trail of Tears. Tahlequah was the other location that included four intersecting lines, which happened to be the end point of the Trail of Tears. The routes were almost perfect matches with the ley lines. Despite the winding of the routes, they followed very closely to the invisible lines as though they were actual roads being followed. It was an incredible sight to see.

EIGHTEEN

The Road to Affliction

Having spoken to Gerald and Marvin, I let them know we would be down that weekend. They were both glad to hear we were coming back. I had explained to Marvin some details of the events I had experienced with my last visit, but couldn't bring myself to discuss the entire night at great length. Jared and Snort were free that weekend, so we decided to go down to get some work done and see what might be waiting for us.

On our way down there we discussed a lot of different things. The fact that strange occurrences were happening at home on a regular basis had come up. Snort explained his entire yard being filled with crows shortly after I had left. He explained there had to have been nearly a hundred of them. We joked that it sounded like a scene straight out of

The Omen and he was waiting for Damian to walk around the corner and strike him dead with his glare.

With a quick Google search, we were able to find all sorts of different things a huge number of crows gathered around might mean. There were many different thoughts, theories, and superstitions that popped up. Maybe there was something delicious in my brother's backyard and all the crows wanted a piece of the action. They also could have been there to warn us that something bad was about to happen.

"Well, I guess there's that," I said as we all had a good laugh due to the overwhelming number of things that this little "omen" might have brought us. Secretly every story we laughed off kept adding to the growing list of these things we had all experienced over the last several months.

I called Marvin as we were getting closer and he reminded me that nobody would be at the property until later that evening. He said to make ourselves at home.

After arriving, we piled up some wood at the fire pit. We decided we would go spend some time at Manus Cemetery. I let Jared and Snort know I was going to set up a couple pieces of equipment in the house before we took off.

As I made my way up to the house, the previous trip came flooding back over me. I could feel the countless sets of eyes on me, and I could remember every feeling I had while thinking I might not make it out alive. I was immediately on guard as I walked down the narrow hall and leapt into the kitchen, avoiding the caved-in portion of the floor.

"Hi," *[EVP] a female voice said.*
"Hate, Brandon," *[EVP] raspy male voice followed.*

I sat the recorder down on the ledge in the kitchen and announced myself. I asked whatever might be in the house to make its presence known, and then I walked back out. I knew I would be back later that night. I felt claustrophobia wash over me like a cloak of bad energy. The pressure had built in my ears the minute I walked into the house; it was as though the house was about to swallow me whole.

We headed to Manus as the sun nestled behind the hills. Darkness blanketed the foothills in the blink of an eye. As we approached the humble cemetery, we all felt the thick energy that surrounded the place. It had become common to find ourselves just standing in awe as we soaked in the surroundings. To look at it, Manus seemed to be just another resting place. To feel it was on a different level than most places any of us had ever been.

"Jesus, buddy, I can't get over it," my brother said as we approached the entrance.

"I know, I don't understand it," I agreed.

We all made our way carefully to the center of the graveyard. We stood there, one person facing in each direction; we listened and watched. There was a deafening silence that had taken over since we arrived—no sounds of animals, wind, or anything else. The lights on the K-II meter suddenly went ballistic.

"SPIRITS." *[OX]*

"HOME." [OX]

"Yeah, this would be a good home for spirits, wouldn't it?" I responded as the words showed on the screen of the Ovilus. "Can any of you tell us your name?" I asked.

"EDNA." [OX]

"FLOWERS." [OX]

"Edna? With flowers?" I repeated the words. "Look around, see if you can find anyone named Edna," I asked Jared and Snort as we all spread out.

After a few minutes, Jared called us over to him. As we arrived to where he was standing, we looked in awe at the headstone.

"Edna Brock," we all read. There was a bouquet of fresh flowers sitting right next to Edna's headstone.

"It doesn't work like this," I found myself thinking out loud. I had never experienced such things in my life like names coming from a device and being able to match them perfectly with our immediate surroundings.

"Something is moving, I feel it, something is," Snort said as he paused.

"Dude, look, look, over there!" Snort pointed to the southwest corner of the graveyard. Jared and I spun our heads to see what he was seeing.

"What!" I asked him.

"A man, he was just walking, just the upper half," Snort said as he began walking toward the corner.

"You saw a guy?" I asked, making sure I understood.

"Shit yes, clear as day, the whole torso, his waist up, all of it," he said.

"DEMON." [OX]

"Buddy, um, did you—" I said, as Snort kept moving toward his mark.

"JAMES." [OX]

The K-II meter lights kept going; they were very erratic. With the Ovilus X and the K-II meter going nuts, my brother kept moving toward the corner as I followed him.

"I haven't ever seen anything that clear; he was right there. He looked like he was walking but I didn't see his legs, then he just disappeared right here," Snort told me as he settled in right where the entity had evaporated before his eyes.

"It just said 'demon' right before it said 'James.' I don't know what to make of that, but I would doubt if James is a demon," I told him as Jared joined us.

"Careful, watch it, hatred," [EVP] a raspy strange male-sounding voice was captured on a recorder.

"No way! Look at this!" Jared stood right next to a headstone and pointed to it. We were amazed to see the name "Jim Smith" on the gravestone.

"James, is this your resting place? Did my brother just see you?" I asked. The K-II lights responded by lighting up.

"Are you happy I saw you, James?" Snort asked, as the K-II lights seemed to respond again.

"Okay, thank you James. Can you please let the lights go out? I would like for you to light up two lights for the answer 'no' and four lights for the answer 'yes.' Can you do that for me?" I asked as four lights came on the meter.

A grumbling sound came through the RT-EVP with a distant howling growl that sounded far away.

"Holy shit, dude, did you guys hear that? Over there," I asked as I pointed to the opposite side of the cemetery, my hair standing on end. They shook their heads to indicate they hadn't heard what I did.

"James, is there something dangerous here?" I asked as four lights came on solid on the K-II.

"Can I see you again, James?" Snort asked as two lights illuminated on the meter.

"Would you get in trouble?" I asked as the lights went out completely.

"James, are you still here?" Snort asked. He was looking for more interaction from his newfound friend. The lights on the meter refused to cooperate any further.

"Please go," [EVP] *man's voice.*

"SALVATION." [OX]

"Do we need salvation?" I asked. There were no further responses.

We were making our way back to the car after things had appeared to slow down around us. As we discussed the events that had just occurred, I saw a solid black shadow dart behind one of the trees at the back of the cemetery.

"STIGMATA." [OX]

"Oh, no, really?" My breath was taken away as I replied with an almost sarcastic tone. All I could ask myself was what was going to come up next.

We watched the back of the cemetery for several minutes and even split up to walk the area, but nobody saw anything else. I had explained to them that I had seen a black shadow that was similar to the one I had seen in the house several trips in the past, but that one appeared to be a lot bigger.

Snort stopped to set up one of his trap cameras on one of the huge trees, so if James or the shadow might feel the need to make another appearance, we would have something there that might be able to document the appearance. I left a small amount of tobacco near the entrance, said a quick thank you, and we all got back in the car and took a collective deep breath.

As we arrived back at the property, Annette, Gerald, and Marvin had gathered around the fire. We all exchanged pleasantries and hugs and sat around to catch up while we had something warm to eat. Both Gerald and Marvin took a few minutes to fill us in on some of the strange things they had been experiencing. It seemed a lot of what they had to say was similar to past experiences; it was as if the spirits had a particular way they wanted to communicate with them.

"That cemetery is right out of the 'Thriller' video, it's incredible. I saw a freaking dude!" Snort said, trying to wrap his mind around the experience. We all laughed. It seemed as though everyone had come to terms with the fact that there was no way to anticipate what might happen or when it might happen. We all knew something else could happen at any moment.

We had decided that night we would spend a lot of time conducting on-camera interviews with all three of our hosts to document their personalities, memories, and experiences. We went ahead and set up the camera and asked them all several questions. Everybody was in a very relaxed state of mind, although whenever I peeked over at my brother, he seemed distracted. I knew his mind was still back at Manus on "James." I couldn't blame him. I had seen things on the property and at Manus that kept me up at night. He decided he would venture into the house alone, as he had not really spent much time in there on his own.

Snort's Solo Trip— Developing an Understanding

Just a few days prior to the trip, my brother called me, letting me know there had been some very strange things going on around his house. Aside from seeing his entire yard filled with a murder of crows, he had also seen a lot of shadow activity all throughout the house. There seemed to be awkwardness to the air everywhere he was, especially when I was around.

Snort approached the house with recorder in hand and could feel the eyes all around him; they felt as though they cut deep into his soul. With each step closer to the house, each crunch of leaves beneath his feet, he could feel something vengeful peering at him.

He entered the house and made his way into the kitchen where he saw a white mist moving all along the floor. He snapped a couple pictures with his camera, but nothing showed up as he reviewed them. A familiar feeling of dizziness and lethargy came over him.

"Is that you?" he asked. "Did I just see you?"

He turned on the Ghost Box and it began scanning the frequencies with pops and buzzing noises; for a few minutes there was nothing. He felt sadness come over him for no specific reason.

"Who's here? What can I do?" he inquired.

"Get out!" [GB] An angry voice came through.

"I can't just leave; you know that. Who are you?" He asked.

"Pray; sins; final," [GB] said the same angry voice.

Snort was listening to the voice as a cold chill filled the room. He stood under his blanket of sadness, "I hear you. Tell me who you are," he continued.

"Danger; release; demons." [GB] Again the voice came through loud and clear.

"Was that you I saw when I came in?" he asked.

"Omen." [GB]

Snort's phone began to ring; he had forgotten to turn it off before he entered the house. It was his wife Jenn calling.

"Wife." [GB]

"Holy shit, what the hell is going on? Tell me who you are!" Snort asked.

"He's coming." [GB]

"Who?" He asked.

"Remember, he took things and hits; rape." [GB]

Suddenly, Snort felt something crawling up both legs and was frozen with panic. He was overwhelmed with emotion and was beginning to feel more and more unsafe as the seconds ticked by.

"I'm Beast." [GB] An evil sounding voice came from the box.

"Jesus Christ, slow down dude, let's talk about this," Snort attempted some levity.

A laughing sound came from the box as a thump came from the living room area, making Snort jump.

After a couple more minutes, Snort decided it was time to start wrapping up his unaccompanied trip into the house. As he was beginning to gather his things to head back to the group, Marvin approached the house and came through the side entrance.

"Anything going on?" Marvin asked as he entered.

"Ha! I may throw up. This is ludicrous," Snort said, happy to have some company.

Snort explained to Marvin what had been happening. They both noticed that when Marvin entered the room, the K-II meter started to act up. It had been dormant to that point. When he entered, it fluctuated from three to all five lights. Marvin told Snort he could feel the chill and heaviness in the air.

"Satan." [GB]

Their conversation had been interrupted by an ominous voice. They were both speechless as bad intentions filled the air.

"*DEMON.*" Ovilus X spoke its first word since Snort had entered the house.

"You want to fight me? Have you been scratching me?" Marvin asked.

"*Fun,*" *[GB]* a seemingly entertained voice came through the box.

Everything calmed down after a few more minutes. Both Snort and Marvin discussed their lack of energy. Everybody that had experienced the activity in the house knew that walking into that house was like walking into a ring to face a ruthless opponent. By the time most people exited the house, they felt like they had just gone several rounds with someone or something very strong and very angry. They decided to head back out to join up with the rest of the group.

Campfire Discussion
While Snort was in the House

One question and answer that really stood out during our first interview was when I was addressing Marvin: "In your heart, what do you believe is going on here?" I asked him.

"Purgatory," Marvin looked me in the eye and told me without hesitation and with conviction in his voice.

"So you feel like there are souls trapped here?" I followed up.

"Yes, I have no doubt there is something else here too, but I feel like it's purgatory," he continued as Gerald's upbeat mood suddenly became sullen and all our hosts nodded as though Marvin has just pinpointed something significant.

We sat and talked about the chance that there were multiple souls trapped on the property due to its dark and violent past.

"It's like those poor girls we saw at the cemetery. They got burned up in the house that was a meth lab. Those poor babies were just in the wrong place at the wrong time," Gerald said. We had come across the very modest headstones of two little girls that had both died in a fire.

"So you think it's everywhere, not just on your property?" I asked both Gerald and Marvin.

"Yes, absolutely!" was their response. They knew their property was different and in some ways special.

The depth of the conversation had me creeped out. There were constant reminders that the people, their families, and their ancestors had all dealt with darkness for years far beyond any of our own combined. There were times that the reality of the situation slapped me in the face. They had waited their entire lives for the opportunity to tell the story of their journey as a family from one generation to another. They did not want a detail missed.

"Look!" Jared pointed into the woods as everybody looked at a glowing ball of light that was weaving through the woods.

"What the—" I couldn't complete my sentence as we scrambled to point as many cameras at the woods as we could.

"There!" He pointed over toward the woods behind the house. There were five or six different sets of glowing eyes that seemed to be looking in our direction.

"Go or else," [EVP] a scratchy voice came through a recorder.

The ball of light disappeared within seconds; it was impossible to track. Judging from the distance it seemed to be from us, it may have been as big as a basketball. Jared and I slowly made our way toward the faint glow that was coming from behind the house in the tree line.

"Shh, slow," I told him as we all crept across the yard.

We were unable to take our eyes off the glowing eyes as they disappeared as quickly as they had shown up. There was nothing to see except the blackness of the woods.

We made our way slowly back to the fire where Annette and Gerald sat and waited. They were very quiet when we arrived.

"Where did Marvin go?" I asked.

"He was heading up to the house. That is the light I have told you about several times," Gerald said.

"The one that used to chase people across the fields?" I asked him for confirmation.

"Oh yeah, just like that. I'm glad it's gone. I need to go to my house. This shit is spooky!" Gerald said as he laughed.

Jared and I sat back down to talk with Annette and Gerald. I wanted to give Snort a few more minutes in the house without interruption to see if he and Marvin could experience anything.

After about twenty minutes, Snort and Marvin slowly came walking out of the house. They both looked like they had been hit by a truck.

"Jesus, buddy, unbelievable," Snort said as he slumped in his chair.

"What the hell happened?" I asked him.

"A lot, the Ghost Box was going ballistic. Just one thing after another, the same voice over and over, all sorts of shit about demons and danger. It's just stupid active. I saw a mist," Snort continued to explain his experiences for the next several minutes. I told him about the light Jared and I tried to track, but it had been too clever for our equipment. The frustration of the fact that so much of the activity seemed too clever for our equipment was minimized because of the magnitude of the experiences.

After a break, the three of us headed into the house, still marveling over what we had seen. So far, tonight seemed to be one of those nights where interaction was constant. We went straight into the kitchen to make sure the equipment that had been set up was running as it should have been.

Snort suddenly stopped and his demeanor changed quickly. "There was a shadow right there, buddy." Snort was pointing toward the living room.

He made his way into the living room with his recorder and asked a few questions. We heard some subtle knocking that kept coming from within the walls every couple minutes. With the state of the house, the knocking could have been explained by any number of things, so we dismissed it since we could not get it to intelligently interact with us on command.

"It was like that thing just ducked into the living room when we came in. I haven't seen anything else so far," Snort said.

For a few minutes we looked around, wondering if we might see anything else hiding in the dark corners of the house. I felt something strange beneath my feet, far beyond the normal funhouse effect that everybody could feel. This felt different.

"Astral." [OX]

"Alien." [OX]

"The floors shifted. That was weird," I said.

"What the hell is this place?" I asked, hoping for a response.

"PURGATORY." [OX]

"No way," we all said in unison. The Ovilus had just reiterated exactly what Marvin told us a few minutes before.

The K-II lights went on as it sat next to the Ovilus on the shelf.

"TORTURE." [OX]

"ETERNITY." [OX]

The Ovilus seemed to be telling a story. It seemed to have just indicated that Marvin had been right about the notion that the land could be some type of black hole for lost souls. The feeling all throughout the house was very heavy; there was tension in the air, and all three of us felt on edge.

"I want you," [EVP] *the a man's voice was captured on a recorder.*

"How can we be saved?" Snort asked.

"Nobody," [EVP] *same man's voice seemed to let us know that nobody would be saved on the property.*

Jared then jumped away from the hallway he had his back to. All three of us had just heard a deep, guttural growling sound coming from across the hall in the damp room.

I grabbed the K-II meter off the shelf and made my way into the damp room with a recorder in my other hand. As I walked into the room, I saw another shadow in the far corner. It disappeared in an instant.

"I swear I felt the floor shift just now. Like the whole freaking house moved," Snort said without a response from anyone. "Can you tell what is bothering me? What's hurting me?" he continued.

"Your back," [EVP] *the familiar man's voice whispered.*

All three of us were sore and completely worn out. The night had been very eventful and felt very psychological. The place had different approaches to its reign of terror. It seemed the entire location could feed on us in any manner it wanted to. That night it just happened to run the entire gauntlet of options. We had seen things, heard things, and felt things throughout the night in every location we walked. The entity seemed capable of pointing out what our personal sources of discomfort were. Snort had a history of back problems for many years, and after many hours of investigating, the pain tended to set in. With the response that would eventually be revealed, it was clear that he was not the only one aware of his pain.

We were all on edge and the running jokes had ceased.

"Whoa, what the—hold on," I said as I froze while getting ready to leave the house.

"Dude—" Jared paused and stopped in his tracks, as did Snort.

Several seconds passed as we all stood and stared at one another. Our eyes were wide open and the fear in the air easily pierced the blackness of the surroundings. We stood frozen in time, attempting to figure out what the hell we all just experienced. We stood there, speechless statues, waiting to understand.

"Let's go, get outside. This place is going to come down on us," I suddenly snapped out of my trance and felt like we needed to get outside as quickly as possible.

"Go outside—go now—make note of everything going on. Look in the sky, look in the woods, note the wind, everything. Just go! I don't know what just happened, but we need to know," I told Snort as he quickly worked his way down the hall and out the side of the house.

After a few minutes, Jared and I joined Snort outside.

"That was a fucking earthquake, dude; either that was an earthquake or some really crazy shit just happened. The whole damn house just about came down on us," I said.

We got together and decided that we would leave our experience in the dark when we met back up with Gerald, Marvin, and Annette. I didn't want to alarm them by telling them that the entire house just about came down on top of us. As we slowly made our way back to the fire, I searched online for any sign or news of an earthquake in the area.

"How did it go? Anything happen?" Annette asked us as we approached them.

"That house is always interesting. It seems like there is always something going on," I said.

"Oh, would you look at that? *Did you feel that quake?*" Annette read a text message she received.

We confirmed a 5.6 magnitude earthquake had hit not too far from our exact location. Before we could blink, there were reports all the way from Oklahoma City to Kansas City of people feeling the earthquake. It was the largest recorded earthquake in Oklahoma history, and the three of us happened to be standing in one of the most unreliable and shaky establishments we could find when it hit. I found it somewhat odd that the trail of the earthquake and those that felt it followed the exact path we took to get down there.

"For a second, I thought we were done. If that place came down on us, it would have been over. You've got to be kidding me," I said as I stared off into the darkness. I felt irritated and shaken up. It had not been the first time down there that something potentially catastrophic had happened. I wondered if it was just a matter of time before someone got really hurt, or worse. Whatever it was that lurked on the property seemed to toy with us, and nature appeared to be giving us plenty of signs that we needn't only worry about what hid in the shadows.

We all sat by the fire for a little while, and then Marvin asked if we would go in the house with him. We all threw our hands up and decided that there was really no reason to worry at that point. If the house was determined to eat us alive, it was going to happen whether we wanted it to or not.

My mind raced back to the first time Jeremiah and I walked through the house and the living room floor seemed prepared to swallow us. Then I thought about the freaking widow-maker tree branch that came slamming down to the ground as I led my crew into the house. A freaking earthquake had just shaken the walls from every angle, and everything around us felt like it was about to collapse. I felt like I had been marked since the minute I had stepped foot on the property. We sought answers, but we had to consider what the cost might be to find them.

We entered the house.

"Are you messin' with my friends?" Marvin began the line of questioning with a stern tone and Southern drawl. "What happened earlier? Why are you angry? We are just trying to figure out what is going on here."

A growling sound came from the Room of Faces.

Seeing red, completely out of control, I found myself dizzy. I felt pure anger boiling inside. I felt like I could kill someone if I had something in my hands to use as a weapon. I felt like I was dreaming, it was a simple and very angry dream; someone needed to be in pain.

"You okay, buddy?" Snort asked me as we stood outside the house.

"Huh? Yeah, I'm good, I'm light-headed," I told him.

Several people stood by just gazing at me, as though I had grown a second head. I had no idea what was going on.

"What the hell?" I mumbled, pulling away from the grasp of my brother.

"You okay? Dude, that was messed up," Snort told me in a calm voice, "You just went ballistic."

"What are you talking about? I just remember, I don't know, Marvin was asking questions, I got dizzy," I stammered.

What Just Happened?

"We are just trying to figure out what is going on here," Marvin finished his questioning.

I went stampeding into the Room of Faces and threw my foot into the wall several times, not slowing down with each kick. A few items from atop the vanity were thrown across the room with as much force as I could muster.

"What the hell are you doing to us! Kiss my ass, this is bullshit! Show yourself, you son of a bitch!" I said with my foot slamming yet again into the wall. "Quit messing with us! You are just playing games—nobody is here to disrespect you; we just need to know who the hell you are!" Another kick as the wall swallowed my foot.

After several minutes documented by multiple recorders, the blackout I experienced came to an end with a swollen foot, a bruised ego, and a world of confusion. It wasn't until I listened to the audio that had been recorded that I realized exactly what happened. Initially I felt like I had gotten dizzy and maybe blacked out and had my brother help me out of the house. Listening to myself go completely berserk and then being forced out of the house by multiple people was the last thing I had expected. I didn't remember any of it. Listening to something like that happen was terrifying, especially as the leader of the group. I had completely lost control. It was not like someone had too many drinks at a bar and lost control. I was gone for a period of time and nobody, including myself, could say where the hell I had gone. My physical body was on a rampage and my mind was completely absent. There was no good way to absorb the situation. All we could do was hope it would be the last time something like that happened.

We decided to conclude our evening shortly after that. We all sat by the fire for a little while, mostly in silence, making sure everybody was okay. None of us had ever thought so much would happen; even the Allen brothers had come to terms with the fact that experiences unprovoked were very different than those that were sought out.

We gathered up all our equipment and said our goodbyes to our gracious friends.

"You okay, bro?" Jared asked me as we finished packing up the car.

"Yeah, I'm good. My foot hurts like a bastard, but I feel fine," I told him.

During the long drive home, there was very little banter. Jared and Snort slept off and on. I watched the lines pass by one at a time and wanted nothing more than to go to sleep. I had to remind myself that there was an end goal with our project, but I reminded myself that no research was worth a life. I felt a strength within me though; I had faith that all of it was happening for a very good reason. Despite the forces having the upper hand when it came to wits and sheer strength, we had made incredible progress. More and more pieces to the puzzle had seemed to be falling into place. There was a never-ending fascination and fear with the thought of what might happen next. Many people have read terrifying stories, they have watched scary movies; not many people have found themselves in the middle of a reality that was usually kept to the scenes and pages of fiction.

NINETEEN

The Event

MARVIN AND I HAD spoken about getting a larger crew together to bring to the property. It would allow us to get wide coverage at all times from all the places that had been established as important. We had been investigating for quite a while down there, the fall season was upon us, and winter wouldn't be too far behind. I had been in touch with a girl in a bordering state who had an interest in the paranormal and was working in film production. Because my team and I had discussed with the Allen brothers the idea of creating a documentary to tell the story, it seemed like a good idea to invite her down to experience the property. She had never been directly involved in any type of investigation.

We spoke about the unpredictable nature of the property. I wanted to make sure she understood the potential of things happening that could not be anticipated.

"Well, I've never had any personal experiences, so I am excited. I want to get a feel for the property and the people involved. I will just be a witness. I won't really participate in the actual investigation, I'm not sure about all that," Barbara told me.

She was very professional and seemed eager to join us for the weekend events. I made sure to give her a fair warning about what she might encounter. My goal was never to frighten anybody; for all I knew, it would be an uneventful weekend. Knowing all that had happened, I made it a priority to give everybody involved as many facts as I could so they could make sound decisions during the investigation.

The Crew

Jeremiah had established a team he would bring with him that weekend. They all had a lot of field experience and were very excited to experience the place they had all heard so much about. Jeremiah would have Ben and Claire Nichols, Jason Roberts, Leonard Fernandez, and Brendan Brannan (to avoid confusion, Brendan is known as BB in the story).

I would be bringing Jared, Snort, and Jason Buis with me, so there was a pretty large crew heading down that weekend. Barbara informed me she would be bringing a friend with her as well. I always preferred working in smaller groups, but the land was so widespread that it seemed beneficial to have more people to cover more area throughout the night. Marvin let me know he was excited to meet everybody; he liked the idea of having larger groups come down. Marvin and Annette planned a huge spread of food for everybody, and they would have the main yard area ready for anyone to set up tents as they pleased.

The weekend had arrived and everybody headed to Oklahoma from Kansas City, Iowa, and Wichita. Just after noon, we arrived from Kansas City ahead of all the others. We set up as much equipment as we could. We outfitted the house with a few cameras that would run through the night, and we set up the EMF pump in the kitchen since it seemed to encourage a lot of activity the last time.

Gerald, Marvin, and Annette greeted us as usual and we sat around sharing laughs and stories for a little while once the equipment had been set up. Suddenly, Snort appeared from behind one of the vehicles and had put on a full ghillie suit. He had become one with the surrounding forest, including a very hostile looking monstrous mask that looked like a very angry Sasquatch. We all sat laughing and wondering what in the hell he was planning.

Jeremiah and his crew showed up a little while after we did; they parked their vehicles and everybody made their introductions. I spoke with Jeremiah in order to put something of a game plan together for the evening. We wanted to keep it organized because there were a lot of people to account for. Everyone would be broken into smaller groups and remain in communication through the handheld radios.

Everyone caravanned over to Manus Cemetery to see it during daylight. The risks had been made clear to everybody. The energy of the guardians could not always be seen but could be felt at all times within the confines of the sacred grounds.

I took small groups through the cemetery to let them know the things experienced there. Everybody was in agreement that the energy could be felt all throughout the small plot of land. Everybody made mention of the soft ground that encompassed the entire graveyard. There was a distinct feeling, whether it was night or day, that at any moment something might ascend from the ground; it was unsettling for even the most seasoned investigator.

As the final group completed their walk-through of Manus, everybody packed up and headed to their vehicles. As we approached our car, the hoot of an owl came crashing through the silence. We noted the fact that when we had heard the owl on previous evenings, the activity seemed to be consistently at a heightened level. As the owl continued its call, I knew the evening would be very interesting.

The weather that afternoon and evening seemed as though it would be much more accommodating than it had with my previous trip to Tahlequah. Everything was set up for everybody to have an opportunity to see what the location was really all about.

When we all arrived back at the Allen property, we again broke into groups and headed in different directions. Some went on the hike for the caves while others explored the wooded area that surrounded the property. I took a small group at a time through the house and let everyone know some of the stories we had been told and our previous experiences. After everybody had been shown the areas of interest, we reconvened back near the camping area. Jeremiah and his crew got to work on setting up their tents. They all seemed eager to experience some of the claims that came across as ridiculous or outlandish. I had spoken to everyone for at least a brief period of time in a one-on-one setting so I could answer any questions they may have had. The most common thing that had been brought up to me was just how insane so many of the claims seemed to be. I had never worked with a handful of the people that had come down, so I simply let them all know that I understood where they were coming from. I had similar feelings about some of the tales I had been told at one point as well. The stories were taken straight out of the pages of the best and scariest horror novels. A level of skepticism was always welcome, and I wondered if anything might happen on that evening to change some of their minds. I let them all know the word "impossible" had all but disappeared from my vocabulary since I had begun my work in the area. I knew everyone, including myself, had best be careful what we wished for; in the past, the place had exceeded all imaginable expectations. I kept hearing the sound of the owl in my mind; it was like a broken record. I felt like that night would be memorable.

As I walked the group through the house, we made our way into the soggy room that faced the backyard area. I gave everybody the typical "be careful in here" warnings, as the floors were unreliable at best. We made our way in as Jared positioned himself in one of the corners facing the back windows.

"Holy shit!" Jeremiah lost his breath and pointed to the back of the room.

Several people jumped and let out a gasp.

"Roar," the hairy creature spoke as it peeked in through the back window, calmly raised its camera to point inside the house, and began snapping pictures. He also pointed his camcorder through the broken glass to make sure every reaction was commemorated.

"How do you like it?" the hairy beast said.

"Son of a bitch," Jeremiah said as everybody began laughing.

"Welcome to Oklahoma everyone, and welcome to our crew," I said as Jared and I lost our composure. Snort made his way around the corner and into the house.

Once our little tour had ended and all wisecracks had been made, everybody met back at the campground near the fire pit.

Everybody had nearly completed setting up their overnight dwellings when Barbara and her friend Mitch showed up. I greeted them with our hosts by my side, and we all said our hellos. I offered to take them on a tour after they got settled for a few moments and had a chance to meet everybody.

"Awesome, this place is so cool looking!" Barbara said.

"Yeah, it's pretty impressive. Follow me, I'll take you up to the house. Jason! Come on, dude," I called Jason over, as he had been the person in contact with Barbara before she and I had spoken. We began to make our way toward the house. I let them know that we had some equipment already running inside so mark any shuffling of feet or whispering when possible.

"They're coming," [EVP] female voice

Several seconds of chuckling commenced in the kitchen as our voices could be heard approaching from the outside. [EVP]

I crept slowly into the side entrance of the house as they followed. I settled in the kitchen area since it was the largest open space in the home with sure footing. I explained the EMF pump first, because people can be hypersensitive to the energy put out in waves by the device. I let them know the side effects that might occur when being subjected to the energy for an extended period of time.

The four of us carefully made our way to the back room. Barbara mentioned she felt rather drawn to that room and was not sure why. The K-II meter almost immediately started lighting up. Because of the EMF pump, there was a light almost constantly on; the meter was picking up on the energy being pumped throughout the house. All the lights came on strong as I stood next to the windows that looked over the backyard area of the house.

"Get her," [EVP] female voice

"Look!" Barbara reacted to the meter in my hand that was fluctuating between three and five lights.

"Keep in mind, this meter picks up the energy that the pump in the kitchen is putting out. I am about twenty feet away from it, so it really should not affect the meter too much. Typically the EMF all over this property is very flat; we rarely get fluctuations, so when they start going nuts like this, it is a good idea to pay attention," I explained to our guests.

"So are you trying to interact with us?" I asked as the lights all came on briefly before they all went out. "Okay, cool, but I will need you to do something specific for me. I will need you to light up three lights on the device for the answer 'no' and all five lights for the answer 'yes.' Can you do that for me?" I finished as five lights came on.

"Whoa!" Barbara was impressed.

"Do you know any of us?" Jason said as five lights lit up. "Cool. Do you know all of us?" Five lights illuminated for several seconds before going out.

"How would you know me?" Barbara said, "Do you know my name?" She asked as five lights came on.

"Barb" [RT-EVP] a whispery voice said.

"No bullshit, I am pretty sure I just heard your name." All five lights came on the device as soon as I finished my sentence. "So I did. I heard someone here say Barbara's name?" I asked. Five lights came on again.

"Do you like the fact that all these people are here tonight?" Jason asked.

Three lights came on the meter and held for several seconds before going out.

"So you would rather we all pack up and leave?" Barbara asked as five lights lit up.

The responses stopped completely after a few more minutes of questions. The meter fell completely flat. As we were about to finish up the tour of the house, *"Bunny" [OX]* rang out in a robotic voice.

"Bunny? What in the hell are you talking about?" I asked as the word came from the previously silent device. I noticed the color leave Barbara's face immediately. "Are you okay?" I asked her.

She looked like she was about to cry, "My grandmother is Bunny, she just died two weeks ago. We were really close," she told us as we all paused, wondering if the word might have been something other than a coincidence.

"Are you talking about Barbara's grandmother when you say Bunny?" I asked as all five lights came on strong on the K-II meter.

"Okay, okay, I'm leaving," Barbara stammered as she headed toward the hallway; Mitch followed her closely as Jason and I stood in the kitchen just looking at each other.

"Holy shit, dude," I said in a soft voice as Jason nodded.

"Bitch," [EVP] a familiar female voice said.

Jason and I headed out of the kitchen and followed Barbara and Mitch out the side door. It was a good time to get back to the camp area to regroup. It was still the middle part of the afternoon and people were already getting freaked out.

"Bye-bye," female voice accompanied with chuckling [EVP]

As we all made our way back to the campfire area, Jason took a few moments to speak with Barbara and Mitch; she was clearly shaken up and on the verge of a meltdown. It came to light that she had epilepsy, and she was beginning to feel as if there might be a seizure coming on. I spoke with Barbara and Mitch and they decided it would be best to go ahead and leave. She did not seem to be right since the minute she walked into the house and I had no idea what else might happen on that evening. I also thought the EMF pump inside may have had a bad effect on her. Many people react negatively when subjected to too much EMF, so we all said our goodbyes and thanked them for coming down.

Shortly after the two departed, everyone else came together at the campsite to discuss what had happened. The sun would abandon us within the next hour or two and darkness would settle in. We all wanted to get out and explore a little before we could no longer see without lights. Everyone headed out in small teams in different directions. The day took a very quick turn on everybody, no matter what direction they headed in. All investigators involved recalled their stories and were able to give their points of view as a team; the land would tell simultaneous stories in all corners and would give everybody exactly what they came for. Their experiences would speak for themselves.

The House: Jason Roberts, Leonard Fernandez, and Two Others

"Dude, I seriously just saw a shadow bolt from the backyard into the side of the house. Let's get in there," Leonard gathered up Jason Roberts and a few others as they headed into the house.

As the crew settled into the kitchen, they named themselves so the running recorders could note how many people there were and in what rooms they were located. Leonard stepped carefully into the back room. He and another investigator stood carefully on the soft floor as he decided to attempt communication.

"I feel like something is watching us from outside," Leonard said as he pointed out the window, peering into the backyard. His coworker nodded in agreement.

"Can you make a sound just to let us know you are here with us?" Leonard asked politely.

Knocking and a bang immediately followed his request as Leonard and his fellow investigator staggered backward.

"Damn, all right, can you knock once if you are male and twice if you are female?" Leonard continued.

Knock, knock. Distinct knocking sounds came from an old dresser a few feet in front of both investigators.

"Are you attached to the Allen brothers?" Leonard asked.

A growling sound came from the closet next to the dresser.

Leonard and his partner both froze. They were staggered at the immediate and intelligent responses they were receiving. They made their way into the kitchen area to join Jason and the other investigator present as Jason paused.

"Shh," Jason tried to bring everyone to a halt with their movements and voices. "Do you hear that?" he said in a low, gentle tone. Everyone nodded to the obvious sound of footsteps coming from the Room of Faces.

"There!" Leonard said excitedly as he pointed toward the Room of Faces. "Go! I saw a shadow!"

Jason and one of the other investigators took a few steps into the room as Jason saw the shadow disappear into the inaccessible room toward the backyard. They were stunned; they recognized how rare it was for multiple people to see and hear the exact same thing in a sequence of events that lasted more than a few seconds.

"What the hell, man," Jason said in the direction of the remaining investigators in the kitchen. "That was a shadow, clear as day. The sun hasn't even completely set yet—" he stopped in mid-sentence.

We could hear footsteps running in the backyard area, shuffling through the leaves on the ground.

Everyone stopped at once to listen to the footsteps that sounded as though someone was sprinting through the backyard. Leonard, being closest to the exit, ran outside as quickly as possible to see if he could see anything. Leonard, known for being very skeptical of everything during an investigation, was shaken by an unseen force that seemed to be slapping everyone in the face. He stood in the backyard, surrounded by the woods, and could hear several whispering voices surrounding him. A sense of panic set over him, as he had just experienced a series of events that were simply undeniable.

Leonard was overwhelmed; he was soon joined in the backyard area by his fellow investigators. They all felt surrounded.

"You all right? We kept hearing footsteps inside, but the last few minutes have been quiet. They seemed to keep heading to the back area," Jason said to Leonard.

"Something isn't right," Leonard said.

All four investigators suddenly brought their attention to the same section of woods. The footsteps were violent, and the distance between them and the footsteps narrowed quickly. They were being rushed by something. All four of them jumped back as though they anticipated being tackled by a raging football player. Suddenly the steps stopped completely. All four of them stood without movement or speech.

They made their way back to the campsite at the agreed-upon time. Annette and Marvin were back at the site tending to the fire. The small group shared their experiences with Annette and Marvin as they listened intently. The sun was almost completely gone, but that group already felt like they had been hit by a freight train of activity.

Jeremiah and Brendan Brannan (BB) made their way out of the woods at the far end of the driveway, near Gerald's house, and they began hustling toward the campsite.

"You aren't going to believe what we just saw," Jeremiah said to the crew that had been at the fire for a few minutes.

"Yeah, same here," Jason said with a chuckle.

"I told y'all, it's impossible to explain. It never stops, day or night," Jeremiah said as he attempted to catch his breath.

The Woods: Jeremiah and Brendan Brannan (BB)

Jeremiah decided to accompany BB into the woods since he was very involved in the community of hunting for Sasquatch. There had been a ton of reports all around the area that led them to believe it was worth looking into. They followed the old, overgrown wagon trail that led to the property line. They trekked deep into the woods and kept their eyes out for any telltale signs of creatures that might be lurking in the forest. There were a variety of species of wild animals in the foothills of the Ozarks, so they were careful to keep their heads on a swivel in case they stumbled across any potentially lethal predators.

"You can seriously feel it—like you are being watched from all directions. It's freaking creepy, dude," BB said. Jeremiah nodded.

"Yeah, it's crazy, it never stops," Jeremiah replied.

"There, look at that! Let's take a look," BB pointed off the path where there were several trees leaning in an unnatural manner.

They approached the area; they noticed a couple of the trees had scratch marks that were ten feet or more high. It stood out as odd because of the depth of the marks, and the height at which they were. It looked as though something was digging into the tree, but they knew it to be rare for an animal to do such a thing at that height. They both began scouring the area for any other clues. The fear at the time was the potential for a very large bear or possibly a mountain lion to be nearby; both animals were known to inhabit that area of the Ozarks frequently. It would have been rare to find a bear that stood over ten feet tall though; most of the bears in the region were much smaller.

As the search continued, both Jeremiah and BB noticed a couple different clusters of trees bent in a way that looked as though there was some type of shelter being made. There was one larger than the other, but both included trees bent in a way that would provide cover from everything surrounding them.

"How cool is this!" Jeremiah said.

"Seriously, the scratches and the structures, this is textbook Sasquatch stuff, dude," BB told him.

The ground was difficult to see; there were a lot of leaves on the ground that had fallen in the fall months. As they made their way back to the path, BB noticed a large imprint near a muddy patch along the path.

"Holy shit, no way," he said.

They both stood over the print and regretted not having a casting kit with them. They studied the print and took as many pictures as they could. The impression in the ground was somewhere between a foot and a half and two feet long and appeared to be of a bare, bipedal foot. One of the toes appeared to be broken, as it was shaped in an opposite direction for the foot it would have belonged to. They took turns putting their feet next to it, and neither of them came even close to matching the length or width of the massive print.

After several more minutes of looking around and investigating, they decided to make their way back to the campsite so they could share what they had found. The rendezvous time was quickly approaching. There was an entire night ahead, and at that point, they had no idea what might happen or what they might witness. They worked their way back through the woods to the faint trail and quickly made their way back to the camp where they saw Leonard, Jason Roberts, and several others already settled in.

The Caves: Brandon, Jared, Jason Buis, and Snort

Jared and Snort had yet to experience the caves, so the four of us walked down the steep hills and along the creek bed to find ourselves faced with the large cliffs ahead.

"Whoa, this is awesome!" Snort exclaimed.

We made our way across the slick rocks as carefully as we could so we could climb into the caves to explore. Jason Buis had mentioned before that he felt like the caves might be the hiding place of all sorts of lost history. We had it in our minds that we would go ahead and see if we could find any evidence of his theory while we had some daylight left.

As we climbed into the caves, we all recognized the fact that there was evidence of people there. There were carvings in the walls of the caves of initials and other scribbles. Jason and Snort made their way back toward the back of the cave as it narrowed and they noted that there was a lot of loose rock that seemed to be strategically placed as though it was being used to block whatever was on the other side.

"Seriously, we need to dig back there. I guarantee we would find something," Jason said.

"No doubt, damn it. Next time I'm bringing digging gear and a metal detector," Snort replied.

"Brandon, danger." [EVP]

"I don't know, I just don't feel a lot going on down here for the most part. I wouldn't be surprised if all kinds of stuff might be buried back there though," I agreed.

A growling sound came from a narrow opening to a cave that was not accessible.

"Um, dude," Jared looked at me as I looked back at him, "You heard that, right?"

"How the hell would I have not heard it," I said with a sarcastic tone to hide the fact that I almost pissed my pants.

All four of us confirmed we heard the growl come from just beyond a very narrow wall that we could not fit in. We quietly attempted to decide what kind of growling sound it resembled, agreeing it sounded like a cat.

"Dude, I'm not here to mess with a mountain lion," Jared said.

"Nope," Jason and I echoed each other.

"I didn't bring my .40, shit, not my day," Snort said.

We decided that our machetes would very likely not get the job done if we had to fend off a giant cat. We decided to head back to camp; we were just a few minutes from the time we had agreed to meet up with everyone at camp. The feeling of being watched was obvious and our sense of paranoia was at an all-time high; we felt like at any moment we could be shredded by something a lot faster and more nimble than we could ever hope to be.

As we got back to camp, everybody was back and sharing their experiences throughout the day. I let everyone know about what we had heard down in the caves. There was a very real possibility that if anybody decided to venture down there that evening, they could be walking right into a trap that might involve some type of very large predator. I suggested that spot might be best left for another day. A couple of the others said they might go down there later, depending on what was going on. Aside from all the very real and frightening experiences everybody had, we all had accepted that the dangers did not start and stop with the unseen forces that may be stalking us.

Nightfall

Once the sun abandoned us for the remainder of the night, everybody split into their groups again to continue as we had earlier. I decided to spend much of the evening on some interviews we wanted to film with Marvin, Gerald, and Annette. My group went from one place to another as the night wore on. There was one report after another rolling in over the radios that were scattered all over the grounds. The fall was in full swing at that point, so there was a chill in the air settling over all of us. There were several perspectives being sent in and I spent a lot of the evening documenting and taking notes on all of them. The activity had everybody on edge—it seemed as though the energy never slept and never waned. Its persistence was remarkable.

Manus Cemetery— Leonard and Ben and Claire Nichols

"So Brandon had a lot of stories about this place. We need to keep our eyes and ears open," Ben finalized his briefing with his wife, Claire, and Leonard.

"Wouldn't you think cemeteries would be less active than most places, considering they are the final resting places of people?" Leonard thought out loud.

"Well, with everything I've heard about this place, it may be different. Make sure you don't stomp all over the graves," Ben said.

"Easier said than done," Claire said with a chuckle as the three ventured through the gate of Manus and entered into the graveyard that seemed to be pulled straight out of a well-made horror movie.

"*Hey, Leo.*" [EVP]

The three-person crew went on with their questions as they ventured through the cemetery. Several minutes had passed and the three were wondering if they might not encounter anything at all.

"Are you hiding from us?" Leonard asked.

"Maybe," [EVP] a direct response to Leonard's question.

"Are you the one that showed yourself to Brandon and his friends?" Leonard continued.

"No," an audible voice said. *[disembodied voice (DV)]*

"Whoa! Did you guys hear that?" Ben asked. Leonard and Claire both took a deep breath and confirmed they did.

"If that was you speaking, can you please make another noise so—" Claire was interrupted.

A loud screaming sound came from the back area of the cemetery.

All three jumped at the overpowering wailing sound. With their heart rates skyrocketing, Claire continued her line of questioning, "Can you tell us where James is?"

"I don't know where James is at," [EVP] immediate response unheard by the investigators' ears as it occurred.

Ben attempted to contact Jeremiah back at the campsite because things seemed to be slowing down; he was looking for some guidance as to where exactly James was located.

"Look!" Leonard said in a stunned voice.

All three of them stood in awe as they looked back to one of the corners of the cemetery and saw snow gently falling. They slowly approached the area.

"Not possible. There is nothing anywhere else," Ben hung up the phone as they kept working their way to the spot.

In an area of about six square feet, snow was lightly falling for several minutes, but none was falling anywhere else. All three of them were so perplexed, they needed confirmation from one another they weren't hallucinating. A couple minutes passed and nothing was falling from the sky.

"Here it is: James," Leonard said as the three of them stood where just seconds before it had been snowing—right near James's grave. It was the same grave they had been attempting to find.

"Holy shit," Leonard said as he pointed into the nearby woods just on the other side of the fence. He pointed to two glowing red eyes. All three of them stood and stared at the glowing dots. They disappeared into the darkness.

The trio kept wandering for a little while longer, wondering what might happen next. Things seemed to quiet down; the silence seemed more frightening than the intermittent activity. They started to make their way to the entrance of the cemetery so they could meet back up with everybody back at camp.

"Who's Martha?" Claire asked, noting a name that she had been told has significance in the area.

"I'm Martha!" [EVP] A female voice struggled to get the words out; the response would be found during the review later.

They packed up their equipment and got in their vehicle and headed back. Manus Cemetery had left its mark on another small group of people that had been brave enough to breach its boundaries. They drove away leaving a dust trail, knowing they all just had some very unique and inexplicable experiences.

Back at Camp: Entire Group Present

Back at camp, everyone gathered for a discussion about their experiences that evening. By that time, my group needed to think about packing up and heading back to Kansas City since most of us had places to be the following morning.

"Thanks, everybody, for coming down. Please be safe tonight. Don't forget about all the things with big-ass claws and sharp teeth that might be out there besides any of this other ridiculousness!" I told them as we all chuckled.

Everybody said their goodbyes as we packed up and headed down the road. Jeremiah and his crew agreed to keep documenting everything, and they would push through most of the night to see what else might happen.

"Anybody want to head back down to the caves?" Jeremiah asked his crew. Most of them replied affirmatively, but only a small group would head back down. Jeremiah, Leonard, and BB headed back down into the darkness. They were on high alert, but they felt a trip down there would be productive.

The Caves: Jeremiah, BB, and Leonard

"Damn, dude. I guess it's normal, but the second the sun went down tonight the entire area felt like it came to life," Leonard said.

The three climbed up into the largest of the caves, which happened to have been the cave right next to the crevice the catlike growl came from earlier. Leonard tossed a rock back through the crack as hard as he could to see if there was any response. They didn't hear anything; they all whacked some sticks against the wall of the cave as well and got no response.

They settled in for several minutes, looking around outside to see if anything stood out. They hadn't noticed anything out of the ordinary, so they proceeded to ask a few questions.

"If I take a rock with me from this cave, are you going to be pissed off?" Jeremiah asked.

"*No.*" *[DV]* All three of the men in the cave heard the immediate and intelligent response.

They followed up with a few more questions along the same line, hoping for another response, but did not receive one.

"Are you children? Or little people?" Jeremiah asked, breaking the silence.

"*I don't know,*" *[DV]* the childlike voices responded in a sarcastic sounding tone, as though these spirits were playing a game with them.

"What the hell was that?!" Leonard responded.

All four of the investigators were stunned by what they had heard. They described the voices as something that came straight out of a horror movie: children mocking what they were there doing, yet giving them exactly what they asked for.

They sat a little while longer asking more questions, but they were not receiving any responses, so they decided to get their things together and head back up to the campsite.

"Do you know the guy that comes down here all the time?" Jeremiah asked.

"HATE BRANDON," *[EVP] a forceful voice was captured on a recorder.*

The four brave souls made their way through the thick woods and darkness to get back to the camp. They were all freaked out by the childlike voices they heard ringing through the darkness.

The Woods: Jason, BB, and Leonard

Jason Roberts and BB were chatting with Leonard as they stood near the circle drive at the far end near Gerald's house. The conversation was suddenly interrupted by a loud, howling scream that came from deep in the woods down the circle drive near the abandoned house. Everybody had frozen. After a few seconds, a second and almost identical scream was heard coming from deep in the woods.

"Are you serious?" Jason was rattled.

The three of them headed into the woods in the direction of the scream as quickly as they could, feeling as though they were not only being watched, but being followed. They could find no sign of anything moving in the woods, but they found more prints that seemed to be fresh. The three of them stopped and the sound of steps in the woods stopped too. They knew they were being stalked. With every step they took, there was a step just a few feet beyond the surrounding veil of darkness. They stood there, feeling that at any moment they might come face-to-face with whatever was creeping around them.

As a rabbit leapt from the brush, all three of them froze, anticipating a collective heart attack. Hysterical laughter ensued as the rabbit scurried off into the darkness. It seemed as though they were being followed by a rabbit, so they all took a deep breath and gathered their wits. They settled down as they enjoyed mimicking each other's deathly scared reactions. After a few more minutes, they began to make their way back to the yard area when the footsteps they had heard before continued. They were being stalked by something other than a rabbit, so the unsettling feeling sunk back into their minds yet again. They knew they were not the only things walking through the woods with the rabbit.

The group met up back at the campfire where they had all pitched their tents; they came to a consensus that they were ready for some rest. They had all heard the screams that had come from the woods, and it had shook things up. Nobody saw anything moving when they investigated, but Jason, BB, and Leonard shared with everybody the fact that they kept hearing footsteps in unison with their own in the woods.

Nighty Night: The Camp
Everybody had nestled into their tents, except Jeremiah; he decided that his best course of action for the remainder of the

evening was to curl up next to the fire. Jeremiah wasn't afraid to get a little dirty, so he lay down next to the smoldering embers of the fire to get some sleep on what had become a frigid night. There were a couple two-person tents set up, and some people had set up their own tents and would sleep alone.

Some of the campers drifted off to sleep. Others were not so lucky. Leonard, a notoriously light sleeper, documented his experiences throughout the night.

After being asleep for a little bit, Leonard was awakened by a very large thump on the outside of his tent. He popped up in his sleeping bag and looked around. The glow of the fire outside the tent cast a huge, dark shadow as it moved from one tent to another and seemed to rustle each one with a violent shake. The shadow slowly made its way around the camp, one shake after another. Leonard peeked out and saw nothing. He only saw the shadow through the tent using the reflection that the glow allowed. In the blink of an eye, the shadow was gone. Nobody else around camp seemed to react to whatever just happened, so he attempted to let it go and get back to sleep.

After what seemed like just a few minutes, Leonard was awakened by more thumps. They were much more subtle. It was as though his tent was a glove catching a baseball being thrown.

Thump; thump; thump; crack!

The thumps were disrupted by the sound of a large piece of wood slamming into another large piece of wood. It sounded like it came from the forest.

Loud growling sounds came from the tree line.

Leonard then heard rustling nearby and slowly unzipped the door to his tent. As he poked his head out, he saw Ben. Several of the investigators emerged from their sleeping quarters to discuss the same experiences; they had all heard the wood knocking sounds coming from the woods, the sound of rocks being thrown and hitting the tents, and the growling. Jeremiah joined the conversation and confirmed everything; he had heard a lot of it, and said he had also heard heavy footsteps all around camp. Nobody had seen anything other than the large shadow Leonard saw through his tent, but he saw nothing when he peeked out.

The early morning sun began to peek over the horizon. Most of the crew had not slept more than a couple hours, but with the rising of the sun, it was natural to get up and shake off the chill of the night while sitting next to the fire. Everybody had heard things throughout the night—it seemed as if the place never slept.

Before tearing down the tents and packing up, Leonard decided to take one more trip behind the house near the woods. Just about everybody had been drawn back there for one reason or another. He decided to take a recorder and conduct one more question and answer session before preparing to leave for the day.

"What exactly roams in these woods?" he asked.

"Everything." [EVP] An immediate and seemingly female response came through the natural noises produced around him.

Leonard spent several more minutes asking questions. He seemed to receive some responses, but not all were completely audible to determine what was said. In his mind, he was hearing the sounds of nature—he was not hearing what his recorder was capturing at that precise moment. One of the voices he captured sounded very angry and seemed as though it was attempting to explain what exactly it was, but the words were not clear enough.

Native American chanting began; both male and female voices were captured. The chanting lasted for several seconds. [EVP]

Jeremiah joined Leonard behind the house and they decided to go inside to start collecting the equipment that had been running all night. When they got into the house, they took note that some equipment had been run down and others were still running.

"Dude, it seems like whatever is around here really focuses on the brothers, huh?" Leonard said as their Mel-Meter registered strong readings.

Evil sounding laughter came through.

"Yeah, look at that, it seems like mentioning the brothers makes the Mel go crazy," Jeremiah acknowledged.

"I'm back!" [EVP] An angry sounding voice was captured.

They made their way outside after collecting the equipment.

A loud bang and the sound of a woman's voice were picked up on a recorder and caught the attention of the guys.

"Jesus, does it ever stop?" Jeremiah asked rhetorically.

"Seriously, are you a relative of the Allen brothers?" Leonard asked.

"No," [EVP] a woman's voice said.

"You are not allowed to follow us or attach to us in any way, do you understand me? We will come back to see you again, but you cannot come with us," Leonard demanded before getting into his car.

Everybody finished packing their gear into their vehicles. Marvin came to say goodbye, so they all thanked him for the hospitality and climbed into their rides. They caravanned down the dirt road as Marvin watched them roll away. He slowly turned toward the abandoned house, feeling eyes burning a hole into him.

TWENTY

Back Home

Following the trip, it took everybody a few days to recover. I had asked those that went down there to let me know what they had found when they reviewed the data that had been collected. The personal experiences that came flooding into my inbox following the trip were mind-boggling. Every single person had one experience after another.

After several days, I received an e-mail from Leonard, in which he expressed how amazed he was about Tahlequah and how much fun they all had:

"That place is incredible, dude, but some strange things have happened since I've been home. When I got home, I unpacked everything like normal and when I took one last trip outside to make sure I had gotten everything out of my car, I felt like I wasn't alone. This was in broad daylight. As I walked to my house from the street, I suddenly felt like something ran up on me, so I actually started running for my house! It chased me all the way into my house, man; I have never experienced anything like that in my life."

"The next morning," he started, "when I stepped out my front door, I started to walk off my porch and something large and black caught my eye. I looked over to my right, and standing at the end of my property line, something huge and blacker than black seemed to be waiting there for me. It looked like it stood over ten feet tall! It was gone before I could blink. When we were leaving the property, I told it that it was not allowed to follow me and was not allowed on my property. It was like something was standing there wondering if I really thought I could tell it what to do. Honestly, there have been times since we got back that I've wondered what the hell I got myself into."

I was told similar stories by a lot of the people that had gone down there and participated in the investigation. Leonard later reported that his experiences at home went on for months.

He had told me that he felt as though something was controlling his thoughts, behavior, and subconscious since his trip to Tahlequah. In some ways, he had become a different person in the months following the trip. His job was falling apart and he felt like he was in a very dark place that he couldn't pull himself out of. He ended up finding his breaking point and lashed out in frustration, begging whatever energy had taken hold of him to let him go. He was angry, and he told me after he hit that point, things seemed to finally calm down and his life began to turn back around. The black thing he saw only appeared the one time.

Strange occurrences seemed to accompany the trips that were made. People felt different than they normally would, and extraordinary things happened regularly to people that had gone down there. It would be irresponsible to say that it was all something to be considered within the realm of "paranormal," but the location had taught me that there comes a time when coincidence goes out the window and you simply had to document as much as possible and hope that there wasn't something substantial or life-altering to any of it.

TWENTY-ONE

Marvin's Story

AFTER SETTING UP SOME equipment in the house, Marvin and I sat by the fire; it was quiet. We had attempted communication while we were in the house for a little while with limited responses. The K-II meter was responsive once again when Marvin handled it. It seemed as though something within the house wanted Marvin to believe it was a relative of his trying to connect and communicate with him. It was just him and me and we began sharing stories with each other. I had told him about other cases we had worked on and some of the trauma I had to fight through in order to keep doing what I loved to do. He began to open up to me about his personal experiences. I never wanted to push him, I simply reminded him that the more information we had about the past and their experiences, the more pieces to the puzzle could be gathered. With the crackle of the warm fire in front of us, Marvin gazed off into the distance.

"It makes me feel like a crazy person to say out loud, but some of the things I have experienced in my life just can't be explained rationally. I have no proof of a lot of it, but these things happened. I have kept it all to myself for a real long time because I knew nobody would believe me and I didn't want to end up in the nuthouse like my brother." Marvin stared off into space as he poured his soul into my lap. He had never had anybody to talk to; he and Gerald knew a lot of the same stories, but didn't speak of them much. He knew I was a confidant that would not judge him, so he took the opportunity to open up to me.

"Tell me some of the things that have happened," I encouraged him.

"I used to have night terrors a lot when I was a kid. I remember having dreams about being in a strange, scary place surrounded by little creatures. I would see a bright light outside my window, and then the next thing I knew, I was somewhere else and couldn't move. There have been tons of sightings of unexplained objects all over around these parts," he told me.

"You feel like you may have been abducted? Were all these instances dreams?" I asked him to clarify.

"I can't say for sure, but it felt real. I can't count how many times I've seen things while I was wide awake. These night terrors were different. I would wake up with scratches and bruises on me, like I got beat up or something," he continued. "Gerald and Curtis, my older brother, use to have the same dreams. We would be going through something like a tunnel and it seemed like we were traveling a thousand miles an hour. It was like we were traveling through a telephone line. It was real scary, really bizarre. We all had these dreams, which I thought was weird. Usually it seems like dreams are personal, but these dreams seemed to run in the family. We didn't talk about it as kids; we just found out as adults that we shared these dreams."

"Gerald told me the same exact story about the same dream he used to have when he was younger. He said your mom used to tell him to never let go, to hold on as best he could, or he may be lost," I told him. Marvin had no idea Gerald had told me the same story.

"I'm the youngest of eight, so I don't know a lot about what my older brothers went through. They didn't talk to me about a lot of that stuff. I never heard Mom tell me not to let go; it sent me into night terrors and eventually a seizure. When the seizure happened, they said it was like I was possessed by a demon," he told me with his voice weakening.

"No shit? What happened?" I asked, hoping that we might be breaking some new ground about what might be hunting in the darkness.

"The doc had diagnosed me with temporal lobe seizures and put me on a medication, Dilantin, I think it was called. To this day, I honestly don't know if they were really seizures. They said I would have incoherent speech. I would growl and jump out of the hospital bed and try to flush my own head down a toilet. I would always throw up violently, too," he told me.

"I'm no doctor, but those don't seem like seizure symptoms to me," I said.

"Me neither. A while after all that, the doctor eventually told me he thought I was losing my mind. After I was about thirteen, I never had a seizure again; I flushed the meds down the toilet and refused to take them. I know, it sounds like the damn exorcist!" he told me with a small chuckle.

"Wow. Then that incident with that girl in the truck?" I asked him.

"Yeah, that was one of the most freaked out I've ever been. I took off. She flipped out and started to change and I just ran for my life. I found out later that she had been possessed as a child. I had no idea it was her. I had heard the stories of the girl that was possessed around here a long time ago," he told me, "Back in the early '80s they weren't that up to date on seizures, and it being in a local Indian hospital, a government facility back then, they didn't have a lot of technology," Marvin said.

"I remember after my first seizure when I came to, Mom was yelling at me. She was yelling and asking what I had been taking and what I was on. She thought I was on PCP or LSD or something," he finished while wearing an uncomfortable smile.

"Holy shit, dude, I'm sorry you had to go through all that. I can't even imagine." I wasn't sure what to tell him. I knew he needed someone to talk to, so I was there with open ears and an open heart.

"Yeah, I could never tell if it was aliens or demons or what. But something had a hold on me that I thought would kill me. I remember seeing those pictures of when I was a baby in that house and there was almost always a black shadow crawling right next to me on the floor. It's messed up," he told me as he flashed his laser up into the air. Just as his laser went out, there were several bright blinks that came from the sky as if they were responding to him.

"No way! What the—" I said as we both saw the lights flashing down upon us.

Marvin pointed his laser up into the sky again as we both watched with anticipation of something responding again. We both confirmed what we had seen, and there was another blinking light that responded within seconds after Marvin flashed his pointer to the sky.

"That has happened a lot of times," he told me.

"That's crazy, there's no source though," I said.

"Not that we can see anyway," he told me as I nodded in agreement.

"I just point the light to the sky and a lot of times there are blinks that respond right back. I remember one time about a year before you started coming down; I woke up one night and it looked like Christmas lights outside my bedroom window. The next morning I could barely get out of bed, like my energy was totally zapped. My face hurt and was really red, like I had bad sunburn or something," Marvin told me, still staring up to the sky.

"So many things around here scare me so badly; sometimes I have to have lights on through the night. It all makes me feel insane. A mind can't fathom what I really know. Even my own mind won't let me fully grasp the things I have seen and experienced here," he continued. "I feel like I've been living different lives, but that goes against my religious beliefs. I have dreams where I feel like I'm living two lives. The life here and my dream life are as real as my conscious life."

"You didn't ask for any of these things. I think you just happened to be born into a place that is really powerful. I have no idea if we will ever know what exactly is here, but I can testify to the fact that you aren't crazy. Everyone that has been here has experienced something along the lines of what you guys have told us. My dreams have been getting worse and worse since I've been coming here," I said.

"Sometimes I feel like I am being watched. There are just reminders all over the place. That creepy feeling or a sound that I hear that can't be explained. Something reminds me it is still nearby all the time. Something intelligent is around me, but why me? It's like it has a grip on me from the inside," he said.

"We are dealing with things that may be as old as time, brother. Can you think of an easier way to mess with somebody than to get into someone's head psychologically? If there are things here powerful enough to get in your head, they could easily make you and other people think that you are losing your mind. That way it can stay in the darkness, hiding, and still ruin you. There have been spiritual things here for longer than we may ever know. Over time, they likely have gotten more and more powerful, so we are no match. All we can do is keep our faith that where there is darkness, there is also light," I told him. "There are thousands of organized religions in the world. I won't pretend I'm smart enough to be able to say which one is correct in its teachings. Who the hell knows for sure? All we can do is hold our faith close to us and know, regardless of which religion we may subscribe to, that if we have faith in the love and protection of good, then we will be okay in the end." I found myself spilling my own soul into Marvin's lap.

"I feel like I found this place for a reason, that's for sure. I don't believe in chance when it comes to this stuff. I have felt connected to you guys since the minute I got here," I told him as he nodded.

"One day, I met a lady in town and we casually talked for a little bit. She told me that we were meant to meet. She asked me if I knew what mind control is. I told her I did. She actually cried when we were talking, as though she was overwhelmed by my presence and my energy. Before we parted ways, she said 'they are messing with you,' although she didn't say specifically who or what she meant. She was from Fort Smith, Arkansas. I only saw her the one time, haven't seen her since," he told me.

"Weird, see man, it seems like people know when they have connected with someone regardless of how long the conversation is or what the circumstances are," I said. "Being down here has already taught me a lot. I know it's likely whatever is here may always be here, but I feel like we all can learn so much from each other and whatever is here. I'm scared to death of this place, but I am also in love with it," I said as I realized the level of crazy my tone and words were likely hitting.

Marvin and I sat around the fire and added a few more logs as the pops and sparks flew up toward the sky before disappearing into the pitch blackness. Being able to share stories and experiences with one another was what the project was all about; at least that is how we all felt. We knew we were there to learn and experience things, but in the end, it was about us as people attempting to connect with energy that nobody could explain. We could sit in silence just gazing up at the endless number of stars, wondering if there would be any more blinking lights from afar. We could simply think about all that had happened to us.

AHHHHHHHHHHHHHHHHHH. An incredibly loud scream almost knocked us out of our chairs.

"Holy shit," I stammered as I got to my feet as quickly as I could and grabbed my bag and recorder and took off down the driveway toward the side of Gerald's house. It had been the most blood-curdling scream I had ever heard, and I found myself running toward it.

Marvin was so rattled he stopped and quickly grabbed a rifle out of his truck as I took off down the driveway. We had no idea what the hell we just heard, but my mind was thinking about the stories I had been told about the screams of the banshee or a stereotypical Native American war cry. I kept running down the dirt road, wondering what I was running toward.

"Recording, Marvin and I just heard the loudest scream ever near Gerald's house," I said with shortened breath into the microphone of the recorder as I finished my sprint that felt like miles.

Please tell me something is running. Did I really just miss that on all these freaking recorders? You've got to be shitting me, I thought to myself as I heard Marvin getting closer and closer. Shortly after Marvin caught up to me, I remembered that I had a recorder running in the house. Even though the house was nearly one hundred yards away, I knew there was no way it could have missed the scream. It was louder than any human scream I had ever heard in my life.

Marvin and I made our way into the woods along the old worn path. We stepped methodically and looked in all directions as we made our way deeper into the woods. We found no signs of people anywhere, so we wanted to make sure nobody was hiding. We searched in all directions. There were a few minutes when we would take a couple steps and pause, only to hear identical steps being taken either in front of or behind us. It was as though our footsteps had a perfect echo to them, as though someone unseen was mimicking our every move. We both acknowledged the sounds as they happened but couldn't see anybody to accompany the sounds. The sounds seemed to be about ten feet from us, so if there had been people, we would have seen them.

We searched the fence line and the woods as best we could for almost an hour, but we saw no sign of any other people out there. I went and knocked on Gerald's door to see if he heard anything. He confirmed he had been sleeping. The only signs of life we could see or hear had to be at least a mile away. We could faintly hear the occasional loud voices and laughs, but they were all well beyond the canyon that surrounded the property. There was no way those voices could have carried with such force over such a distance. We had found nothing; we had only heard some strange sounds in the woods as we navigated our way through.

After a little while longer, we decided to call it an evening and pack up for the night. We kept rewinding the recorder that had been running in the house so we could listen to the scream repeatedly; it floored us every time. Each replay raised the hair all over our bodies. While out in the woods, I attempted to replicate the scream just so I had something side by side to compare the original to. My scream at the top of my lungs was a mere fraction of the power of the one we had captured. My voice did not hold up to the booming shriek on any level. We attempted to analyze it and break down what animals could have possibly made the sound, but we could not think of anything. This did not sound like an animal, it sounded like a human wail.

TWENTY-TWO

John and Brandon

I HAD SPOKEN A few times with a friend of mine that I had previously worked with. He had expressed an interest in accompanying me down to Oklahoma, so I got in touch with him and set up the trip.

John, a member of a Kansas City paranormal team, was a friend of mine and we had enjoyed working together a few times. John and I had a pretty similar approach when it came to our desire to explore the world and see what we could find; we had a never-ending thirst to learn and experience as much as we could.

I enjoyed hearing the stories John would tell me from his travels, and I shared a lot of stories from my past as well—specifically from my Air Force days. When we arrived in the afternoon, Marvin, Annette, and Gerald were there to greet us as usual. We all sat down and John got to know my friends a little better.

As I took John around the property, he immediately noticed the feeling of being watched. He told me that he had felt it from the second we got out of the car. I tried to limit some of the details such as common feelings we had all experienced around here prior to our arrival. I wanted to simply gather information from John as to what he felt and how he would approach the area. I explained the place was typically very active, and there was no way I could possibly explain exactly what to expect; I let him know he needed to be on guard and ready for anything.

The woods seemed to watch us as we walked down the driveway toward Gerald's house. We heard distinct footsteps that seemed to be walking parallel to us as we moved; we could hear the leaves crunching beneath the feet of whatever was moving along with us.

"Dude, what is that?" John asked me.

"Yeah, I don't know, it happens constantly," I responded.

John took a few steps into the woods to investigate and see if he could find the source of the footsteps. I went in the opposite direction to see if we could flank whatever it was and possibly get eyes on it.

"Jesus, what the hell!" I blurted out as a small stone fell to the ground after bouncing off my shoulder. "Dude—I just got hit with a rock," I told him.

"Are you serious?" he said as we both chuckled.

After a few more minutes wandering in the woods, we made our way back to the driveway so we could head down to the caves. I had put the stone in my pocket. I couldn't say why, but I felt I needed to keep the stone that mysteriously struck me.

As we approached the caves, John was in awe of the surroundings. The cliffs were very large but difficult to see through the thickness of the woods until they seemingly appeared out of thin air. We climbed up into the caves and looked around to see if we could find anything that stood out.

"You will feel watched almost the entire time you are down here; it doesn't matter where you are. I just hope it isn't a freaking mountain lion that is watching us," I told him.

"Do you know my friend?" John asked.

"Brandon, go." *[EVP]* A familiar male voice was captured on one of our recorders.

"I just felt like something brushed against me just now," I told John, looking around to make sure nothing had fallen from the cave walls. I was surrounded by rock, but nothing was close enough to have pushed by me.

John and I explored the caves for a little while longer before making our way back to the grounds. We had decided we would go over to Manus Cemetery before sundown.

After we made our way back to the camp, our friends had dispersed but would be back later that evening.

I had taken a walk through the abandoned house before we packed up and headed over to Manus, and John told me a couple different times he thought he had seen a shadow dart around a corner as if to be avoiding us. I set up a recorder in the house so we could have audio running while we were gone.

Footsteps were walking through the Room of Faces and into the kitchen. Mumbling words from several sources, laughing all at once. Knocking on walls, in sets of three, occurred intermittently.

"They need to leave; dead," [EVP] a scratchy voice said calmly as we drove away.

The house seemed to have come to life right after we walked out. As the recorder ran for almost two hours while we were gone, there were many notable sounds and voices that were captured on the recorder. It was as though the house had a pulse and knew when we were gone and when we would be back.

Despite being a very modest place in size, Manus made up for it with an overwhelming force of demeanor. I had not seen anybody approach it without some uneasy feeling.

"Are you kidding me?" John said.

"Yeah, just be careful here. No provoking—tread lightly," I gave him one final warning as we slowly approached the entrance.

"Gotcha," he confirmed, "Dude! The ground is like a sponge! Weird!"

We slowly made our way around the cemetery; I felt like something was off compared to the several other times I had been there. The sun was still shining, although it was quickly making its way over the horizon.

I had set up several pieces of equipment and we went to visit "James," but on that evening, we did not get much of a response. I was not sure what I was feeling, but it was unique to feelings I had there during my previous visits.

"Dude! Back there!" John exclaimed. He picked up his pace and headed to the west fence line at the back of the plot of land. "I seriously just saw a shadow go all the way from over there to behind that tree."

John continued to approach the tree that backed up to the fence; it was as though we were both waiting for the shadow to come bolting out the other side of the tree at any moment. Our senses were piqued.

As though a plow was running through the leaves toward me, I quickly turned my attention to the northwest corner of the cemetery and was left paralyzed.

"John, what the—" I tried to get John's attention as I stood still glaring at the back of the cemetery.

"Hello? How's it going?" I called out to what looked like a man standing and leaning against one of the trees on the other side of the fence.

"What did you say?" John asked me.

"Dude, what the hell—I—I need you to make your way to that corner," I said as calmly as I could while pointing my camera toward the man. There had been no movement or response to my inquiry.

My eyes adjusted quickly as I saw what looked like a man begin to expand. All features were gone in an instant as the being grew and grew; it pushed its way up and stood between two trees and began to sway slowly from side to side. I was completely mesmerized. This creature suddenly looked enormous and as though it was made of mirrors. It was reflective, but didn't appear to have recognizable features. I slowly took one step after another in an attempt to approach the creature.

"Hello? Seriously, who's there?" I asked. The creature continued to slowly and meticulously sway from side to side as it was locked onto me. I could not pick out its eyes, but it needed my attention.

A loud, howling growl came as an EVP over the recorder I had set on one of the tombstones.

"Dude, I can't see, my eyes are watering," John said as he approached the corner of the cemetery, "What the hell is it?"

I took another slow step, still feeling incapable of completing a coherent sentence. I had no idea what to do; all I knew was that whatever the thing was, it appeared to need my attention. It had accomplished just that; it had my undivided attention.

After another minute and a half, the creature bolted in the opposite direction through the leaves; it was as though the plow had left as quickly as it had arrived. I stopped in my tracks and felt like I took my first breath in almost three minutes. I didn't know what just happened. I made my way back to the corner to look around. The sun quickly set and we stood in darkness as I explained to John what I just experienced.

"So you didn't see it? You were only about ten feet away from it!" I said as John explained to me that he couldn't see anything because his eyes had suddenly began to water as he approached the corner.

"Dude, it was insane, I felt really weird and suddenly my eyes were just watering. It was like I was tuned out completely, I was just wandering," John told me.

"That thing was there for a couple minutes. I don't even know how to explain it. I felt like it was in my mind. Like I couldn't see anything it didn't want me to see. What the hell was that thing?" I stood in shock.

A loud howling growl identical to the one before came ringing through as an EVP on the recorder. The sound was in the distance, but was not recognizable as a known animal.

"It was right here, leaning up against this tree," I told John as I mimicked the creature. "It looked like a man at first, then all of a sudden—" I realized the location of the other tree that the creature had been leaning against. I couldn't stretch my arms and touch each tree at the same time. Whatever I had encountered had pushed through both trees simultaneously. It was not only touching those trees but had moved them both at the same time. They were about eight feet apart. I looked up at the area where the creature's head had extended to and estimated that it stood somewhere between ten and twelve feet high. Even when the creature looked like a man, it was well over seven feet high from the base of the tree it had been leaning up against.

We both heard rustling in the woods nearby; it was pitch-dark, so we couldn't see anything outside of where our flashlights extended. We asked a few questions into the darkness and received no response.

I explained to John that as it had approached, it made such an obvious and loud noise that my attention was drawn directly to it. Even if the direction was known, I noted that it was very difficult to immediately find an object when scanning a thick, wooded area. A person's eyes have to scan the area and lock in on an object that is surrounded by other contrasting elements. In that instance, the object that had approached immediately got my attention. My eyes went directly to the creature and locked in on it without having to search at all. It approached, I saw it, and then we had an interaction that I would never forget.

As we walked to the car, I kept looking back as if the creature may be walking right behind us. Something in me felt like it was still watching us. Suddenly, a very distinct laughing sound came from the Spirit Box. The box was not even turned on. It had powered on without being touched and a distinct laughter was coming out of it. We stopped so I could remove the box from the pocket of my backpack. We confirmed it was turned on and there was laughter coming out of it for almost thirty seconds. The channels were not scanning as they normally would have been if we were using the device to attempt communication. The box's power button needed to be held down for seconds before it would even power on. With its small buttons, the device was difficult to manipulate without intention. The instance, paranormal or not, was very eerie after seeing the creature.

As we packed up the equipment to head back to the Allens' property, I reviewed both cameras we had running in the cemetery. Due to the low lighting, and the sunset that had just fell over the horizon behind us, we were unable to capture any visual evidence of the creature that had approached us. I had wondered if it would be best to just pack up and head back to Kansas City. I was trying to wrap my brain around what I had seen and why John was completely incapable of seeing or hearing something so obvious. Despite the natural explanation as to why John couldn't see what I had seen, I had to wonder whether or not the creature had the ability to manipulate us physically. The creature seemed to have wanted my attention, so I wondered if it had the ability to block John from being able to see it.

We arrived back at the land and Marvin was there tending to the fire. We sat down with him for a little while and discussed what we had experienced.

"Could have been a shape-shifter, could have been what y'all might call a Sasquatch, could have been a demon, could have been a lot of things," Marvin said as he recalled countless stories in the area of those types of creatures. "Only medicine men are powerful enough to shape-shift though, but it's possible," he concluded.

"I don't know what the hell it was. It blew my mind though. It was as though it needed my attention—that is what kills me. John couldn't see it and he was just a few feet away from the damn thing," I said.

"Yeah, that makes sense. Why would something like that want a bunch of people seeing it? Those places are sacred and protected, that is for sure. Y'all haven't been stirring up trouble in there, have ya?" Marvin asked.

"No dude, no way, we don't provoke anything in there. We just ask for interaction. We don't press our luck," I said, understanding that our presence alone could very well stir something up that would not be welcome.

The three of us decided to head into the house after we sat for a bit.

Marvin liked attempting to communicate with the spirits by using the K-II meter. We felt very confident that the EMF readings all over the property were nearly always zero unless there was some type of anomaly that created an adjustment in the energy field. We didn't assume that any fluctuation meant there was a ghost, but it made it very easy to attempt to establish a line of communication that was easy to see for all of us, and it seemed to work. As soon as we walked through the door, the meter went off in Marvin's hand.

"So you're here tonight? You fixin' to talk to us?" Marvin began. The lights on the meter began lighting up in order, from the first light all the way to the fifth, one at a time, it was like a wave of light and it repeated several times. I had never seen the meter behave in that manner before.

"Do you remember what we need you to do? Three lights for 'yes' and two lights for 'no'?" I asked as three lights held steady in Marvin's hand.

The lights on the meter seemed to cooperate for several minutes before they went silent. As the lights went dark, so did the feeling in the house.

"I keep feeling cold blasts all around me, like they are circling me," I said, noting that there was no wind on that calm night.

"I got goose pimples everywhere," Marvin mentioned. "Where'd you go?" he asked.

"Go, now!" A female sounding voice came from the damp room in the back.

"Did you just hear that?" John asked as we both nodded.

"Could you tell what it said?" I asked as John headed toward the back room.

John spent a few minutes investigating the back room, but none of us heard the voice again. I had rewound one of the recorders quickly and was able to confirm what the lady's creepy voice had said to us. We decided to get back to the fire. There were some things I needed to discuss with Marvin regarding his personal experiences from years past. We took every opportunity to document all the information they could provide us.

As John and I drove home that night, the car felt cold no matter what I did. There was something out of place around us. There were things I had been told by the Allen brothers that seemed to seep into my soul. I felt overwhelmed while driving; I remembered my solo experience at the property, and I felt at any moment I could get sick again. I looked to my recent blackout, something I had never experienced before; something was wrong.

"*Purgatory.*"

"*They'll follow you.*"

"*They are always watching.*"

Symphonies of reminders were flowing in my brain, and it was palpable all around me. I could feel the energy surrounding me as though I was zipped up inside a sleeping bag, giving me only a small airway to breathe through.

After what felt like days, we finally arrived back home and I could not get to sleep quickly enough.

TWENTY-THREE

Life Happens

EVERYBODY WAS OVERWHELMED WITH the combination of exhaustion and typical things that life brings everybody's way once in a while. The winter had come, so the opportunities to get to Oklahoma had vanished. At the beginning of the winter, I got a call from Gerald.

We talked for a half hour or so, mostly about life. I enjoyed talking with Gerald because he gave me a different and honest perspective. Clearly he was a man that had been through a lot in his life; he had a very curious soul.

"My cancer came back. It doesn't look too good," he said, as though it was no big deal.

"Jesus, Gerald, I'm sorry. I don't know what to say," I was stunned.

"Some scary shit, that's for sure. Doc says it's spreading fast, so it doesn't sound real good. So I am going to start treatment and everything. I just wanted to let you know. I want to see you soon too. You've all been a blessing to us for a long time now. Our paths were definitely meant to cross, I am so happy they did," he told me.

"No doubt, brother. I couldn't agree more. You all are like family to me; I can't thank you all enough for having us down and bringing us into your lives like you have. This only goes as far as you want it to go; I think we have learned a lot about so many things down there over these years. We are friends; we are like family, which is what comes first. Everything else is fine, we can figure all that out," I said. I hoped he knew that the work we had all been doing would have meant nothing if the bonds that had been formed never existed.

Being so close to my friends down there likely allowed the power of the land to sink into me faster; there was a personal attachment to the place. That knowledge could sometimes put me at peace; other times, it horrified me.

"We'll see you soon. Stay warm this winter," Gerald laughed as only he could.

"All right, brother. Be well. I'll be praying for you, stay strong my friend," I told him.

It wasn't long after I spoke with Gerald that I found out I needed surgery on my hip. I felt like my body was falling apart at a young age, and I hoped it would get better following the procedure. I texted with Marvin and Annette regularly. They filled me in on things that had been going on. Marvin had reunited with his former wife and moved away from the property. He went by there occasionally to make sure things were kept up.

The news kept coming from Oklahoma, but it was taken over by the fact that a couple of my brothers were about to move away. The news crushed me because I always had Snort and Jared by my side through everything. There was something so unique about the experiences we had as investigators over the years. As a team and family all in one, we were able to watch each other develop as people. The development was spiritual on an incredible level. We learned to take time to truly care about the world around us and the history of humanity.

Snort, his wife Jenn, and their family were moving to Vermont. Jason had told me that the company he was working for had asked him to relocate to Houston, Texas.

A few months passed. After my surgery, I felt like I would never be the same. The recovery was very slow and difficult to get through, but I eventually felt somewhat normal again.

There were times that the insomnia and nightmares felt like they would be the death of me. When I did finally manage a couple hours of sleep, they were typically spent in and out of some of the most realistic dreams I had ever experienced.

The sins of humanity echoed through the lands. The unsuspecting hills saw a river of blood come flooding over them. As I would awake in a cold sweat, I was reminded that the experiences in Oklahoma were not about the paranormal as much as they were about the treatment of people. I felt as though I was a regular witness to some of the devastation and cruelty that had been bestowed upon indigenous people. All because of differences in cultures and skin color.

The land could never forget the tragedies it had witnessed—no number of years could force the land to forget what it had been forced to see. I realized I had been investigating unexplained activity in an area where war had been raging on for centuries between good and evil.

As I leaned against the back door, still trying to catch my breath—*BANG!*— a huge sound came from just behind me. I could feel the door vibrate against my back with the force of something substantial slamming into it. I felt like I was going to have a heart attack. I thought a tree branch or something had crashed down on the deck and hit the back door. I immediately turned around to see what just happened outside. I saw nothing—everything seemed calm. It was as though nothing out of the ordinary had even happened.

After a few minutes, I mustered the courage to go outside to see if the growling creature was still around. It was completely calm and silent outside. As I went back inside, I felt like something was not right. I had a sudden feeling within me as though something was building. I could feel it from top to bottom; something was happening, unlike anything I had ever felt before. It was then I knew in my heart that the many warnings I had been given and stories I had been told were transforming into something other than merely warnings and stories. There was no doubt in my mind the puzzle pieces were continuing to fall into place.

I wondered if those around me were safe. I now knew why I felt like I was constantly being watched: it's because I was. I didn't know if these were all signs that I needed to flee from the case, or if I was receiving messages and signs that we were about to uncover some long-buried truths. I knew I couldn't stop. Too much had happened to stop short. I needed to reaffirm my standing with my own soul and confirm that I was protected despite being surrounded by such incredibly dark and powerful energy.

As the night wore on, I was incapable of shaking the strange feeling I had. Suddenly my face felt like it was on fire. I immediately made my way to the bathroom—I could feel my skin getting tight. It felt as though my face was melting. I closed the door and locked it behind me, knowing nobody else was in the house. I kept feeling my skin getting tighter and tighter, so I began taking pictures with my phone.

After several minutes, I came out of the bathroom. I knew I had to look at the pictures that had been taken. I was scared to see them, but knew I didn't have a choice. My face felt normal, but as I looked at the pictures I had taken, my heart nearly stopped. One picture after the other, my face was very obviously morphing until my face looked like an angry old man's. It was as though I had aged fifty years in the blink of an eye. I was conscious throughout the entire thing, but I could remember feeling dizzy and confused.

The night wore on; I decided to get some work done because I couldn't sleep. My face had changed for no reason. I knew it wasn't an allergic reaction. I kept looking at the pictures over and over, trying to make sense of what happened. I couldn't even muster a decent theory; I just kept staring at the pictures through the night. I wondered if my mind had found a breaking point; I asked myself repeatedly if I was going insane.

After a few days, I decided to show the pictures to those closest to me. One by one, I showed my brother, then Jason, then Jared—nobody could come up with a logical explanation. I had convinced myself that maybe it hadn't been as obvious as it felt, but with each reaction, I realized the seriousness of what had happened. I just hoped things would not escalate.

I had time to digest all of the strange things that had happened. It had become normal for things to be strange following a trip to Oklahoma. Knocking on walls, doors opening and slamming, and the feeling of being watched were all regular occurrences. I had become desensitized to a point and that scared me as much as what had actually been going on. At what point would I be the one that was haunted, as opposed to the location we had been visiting? Clearly that was the direction things were headed, assuming it hadn't already happened.

TWENTY-FOUR

Picking up the Pieces

IT HAD BEEN A year. The year had been full of highs and lows just like any other; some were exceptional, and others were heartbreaking. There was sickness and loss, loneliness and despair. On the flip side, some of the best things to have ever happened to me in life had happened over the course of that year.

I had been in touch regularly with Marvin and Annette down in Oklahoma, making sure all was well. For a spell, the land had been abandoned. Gerald had been in hospice care for several months; all I could do was hope that the weather cleared up quickly enough for me to go back down to see my dear friend before it was too late. Marvin and his wife were looking to reestablish the land as their home in the near future.

"So you and your wife are looking to stay in Gerald's old house then?" I asked Marvin.

"Yeah, looks like it. He's real sick, not sure how much longer he's got. We've been cleaning up around the place though. It was in bad shape, but we are makin' progress, slowly but surely," he said.

Marvin said much of the activity seemed to have calmed down since Gerald had been gone. It seemed to have gone dormant, but he said it seemed as though something strange was going on in Gerald's house. He could feel it when they had been in there working.

"That's good to hear, at least things are somewhat calm, and do you think a lot of the things were attached to Gerald?" I was afraid of Marvin's answer to my question.

"Yeah, for sure. He's a real personable guy, but he has been involved in a lot of crazy stuff over the years. I think him and his friend made things worse. Since he's been gone, things are pretty quiet," he confirmed.

"Well, there will probably always be something out there, but as long as nothing that feels dangerous is going on, that is definitely a positive. I'm glad to hear it. Have you all looked into that blessing we talked about?"

Getting the land blessed by someone from the Cherokee community was something he and I had talked about on a few different occasions. I felt it was very important.

"Yeah, might be tough getting them to do it with y'all here though. You know," he said.

"I understand. I would love to be there and would love even more to document it as best I can, but I understand," I told him.

I had known that despite my efforts, I would likely never be accepted by the local community because I was incapable of spending as much time down there as I would have liked. I wanted very badly to experience everything I could and learn as much as I could about the people and culture. There seemed to be walls built up that would not come down anytime soon. My main concern was for Marvin and his wife to have peace on the land he loved so much.

"Y'all gonna come down soon?" he asked me.

"Absolutely, I've got a crew ready to go. My brother and Jason won't be there because they moved, but we will be down there the first chance we get. There are a few things I really want to follow up on," I said as we ended the conversation. I was very excited to get back down there; it had been far too long.

I had spoken to Jeremiah, Jason Roberts, and Leonard about getting back down there. We understood that finding all the answers was an impossibility, but we had a really good crew set up to get down there to try and figure some things out.

Over the period of time I had not been going down to Oklahoma, the nightmares had been less prevalent. The feeling of being watched felt like it would never go away. Sometimes it wasn't very bad, but there always seemed to be something keeping me within arm's length. Experiencing the growling noises and seeing shadows in the darkness were still pretty common. There weren't too many times I could remember when I felt completely unsafe though. I experienced something I knew would be with me in my mind and heart for the rest of my life, possibly even beyond that. I connected with something very powerful or, rather, it connected with me. I sought out the darkness and had found it in abundance. I had experienced darkness before, but nothing that felt like a constantly underlying presence. Tahlequah had been with me night and day for years. When I slept, I could hear the screams of pain and anguish. Sometimes they would be so close my ears would ring; other times they would be faint, like the night had mostly swallowed them.

There were a few specific things I wanted to do while we were there. Jared and his friend Ron would join me on the upcoming trek. Jason Roberts, Leonard, and Jeremiah would be bringing a few others with them as well. There was always something in the back of our minds questioning what this place had in store for us. What initially sounded like folklore was now ingrained in us as a reality we had never before comprehended.

The nights leading up to the investigation were becoming more and more restless. There always seemed to be something nearby that made me remember the feeling of being stalked at all times. The dreams had returned. I felt like I could feel the pain within the depths of my mind, which had been burned into me by the land that had seen so much sorrow over many years.

I found myself peeking over my shoulder during broad daylight, and the bags under my eyes presented evidence of my exhaustion before we even went down to Oklahoma. As I peeked over my shoulder, I would see nothing. I could feel the eyes watching me though—I could feel the presence of the energy that had bound itself to me a long time ago.

My thoughts were mostly with my friends, specifically with Gerald. I couldn't comprehend the level of suffering that he had to endure, all leading closer and closer to the end. It is never an easy thing to watch, but I found myself trying to see through the eyes of the afflicted: going for a walk, hearing children laughing, and birds chirping—would this be the last time I smelled the barbecue in the air? The great unknown would quickly be at hand, and when entering into that journey, the knowledge of having to do it alone would have to be terrifying. So many people spend so much of their lives developing and trying to understand their faith in what was inevitable for all of humanity. The question wasn't death; it was how it would come and under what circumstances. The project that had already changed my life also gave me a new perspective on life and death. I had experienced the extremes of darkness and light in the world.

I laid down my head, attempting to get some rest as the trip was fast approaching.

TWENTY-FIVE

One More Step

My friend, come with me, all it takes is one more step and all the pain and misery will be wiped away," a soothing, comforting voice spoke from the shadows.

"It hurts, it just all hurts, I don't know if I can even get out of bed anymore," I said weakly.

The figure in the darkness slowly approached me as I lay in bed. The physical pain had beaten me down and I was exhausted. I was comforted by the presence of the figure. It was dark, but it was as though I was in the presence of an angel. The figure slowly approached me; the warmth and kindness of the figure was easy to feel. I wanted the pain to end—with the pain came the depression. The figure brought with it a calm; there was a feeling of peace in the air. The soothing voice continued.

"Yes, life is pain, but there is a place you can go and forget all the pain. Look around you, there is murder and tragedy in all directions. Come on, my brother, come with me, just one more step."

"My mind won't rest, there is no solitude. I can't escape the nightmares. I am just so tired. I am afraid that I'm losing my mind."

"No, my brother, you are not losing your mind, your mind is simply reminding you that there is nothing left for you here. All the doubt, the stress, the pain, it all goes away with just one more step."

"I can't sleep, I have no energy, and the darkness is constant. Whenever I try to get motivated, something knocks me back down. There is nothing but sadness and despair in my mind. I used to be a happy person. I just don't understand."

"Happiness and true freedom await. There is no reason to be here and suffer through all the pain and misery. Let me take it all away for you. All it takes is you following me, with just one more step."

"I'm going to make today a good day. I am due for a good day. It has just been so cold outside and there is just so much stress all the time. But today will be different. It is all in my head. I am stronger than this. I have a wonderful life. I can put the pain aside."

"Yes you can, and then the pain will return with great vengeance and it will be worse than even it was yesterday or than it will be tomorrow. Your life is pain now. Your life is madness.

Please don't allow yourself to fall into the abyss. So many people fall away and are lost for eternity. Please, my brother, come with me. I can take it all away. There is eternal paradise waiting for you. I have the power to make your wildest dreams come true. Come with me."

"I have so much to be here for. My children, my family, my friends—they need me and I need them. They are my world."

"No my friend, they are their own world. This world is a cesspool and is condemned. Turn on the news if you need a reminder of what humanity has done to itself: famine, murder, genocide, anger, corruption. It's all there in front of you. The world is swallowing itself whole. I can save you; I can save your soul. Walk with me, my friend. One step is all it takes."

"Sleep, I just want a peaceful night of sleep. I feel like I haven't had that in years. My decisions, my calling in life, they have destroyed me. I can't shake the torture in my mind. Please help me, make it stop."

"That is why I'm here, my friend, to make it all stop. You can be well; you can be the happy man you once were. There is nothing left for you here. Come with me to eternity; let me take the pain away. It isn't your fault, they will all understand. How can anybody live here? Humanity has made its decision. Greed, hatred, and corruption in all directions. Nobody should live here. Nobody with goodness in their hearts, such as you, should have to endure such a place when perfection waits. Come with me, my brother, take one step."

"It's cold, I hate the cold. I am aching to my bones. I can hardly breathe because it hurts so much. My mind won't rest. I am beyond exhausted. Please, help me."

"I am here to help you, my friend. The pain, the anguish, it all goes away with just one more step. Don't be afraid, I am here for you and with you. I will never leave you. You are all that matters to me: your happiness, your inner peace. One step is all it takes."

"But if I just push through, there are so many good things going on. I am helping people; I love my family, my friends. My life is so good on so many levels. It's the pain, the restlessness—it just beats me down. I am a strong person; I can get past all this."

"No, my friend, that's why I am here. The pain and the restlessness will never subside. They will get worse and worse as they have already from day to day. You can barely walk now. You can hardly concentrate. There is no need to be like this. You really want to burden those you love with what will remain of you? Please don't put them through that misery and torture. They don't need to ruin their own lives to take care of you like a powerless child. Come, my friend, one more step. Save them."

"No, I will get better. I will be enlightened and strong. I can survive anything. I have already survived more than most. I won't burden them; I will love them and we will all grow together as families should."

"This is why I care so much about you. You are always optimistic, you are strong, and you are selfless. My friend, this is why

I am giving you this opportunity. What you have needed to do here is done. Your kindness and selflessness is too good to waste here. It falls on deaf ears and blind eyes. Come, my friend, just one more step."

"I feel totally powerless; I can't fix anything that needs to be fixed. I can't function like a normal person. There is just so much pain. Please, please help me put the pain aside. I have so much to do, so much to be here for. I can't just leave it all behind. I haven't accomplished everything here; there is too much to do. I need to get going."

"You have tried, my friend, you have given all you can. You cannot even stand up. You are going to throw all the selfless things you've done out and become yet another selfish person? That is not you; you are not selfish like the others. Come on, my brother, come with me. Perfection awaits with just one more step. Do you see the ones you loved that are gone? Do you see them? They found perfection and need you with them. It is time for you to be rewarded; your suffering needs to be gone. Let me help you."

"I'm not selfish, I need to be here. There is so much left to do, so much left to give. The world isn't hopeless; it has rough parts, but there is so much to adore about this world. The beauty, the good—it is as plentiful as the bad and the ugliness."

"My brother, don't lie to yourself. It isn't becoming of who you are. The coldness, the pain, the brutality of the world; these are tangible and real things. You do not need this madness anymore. Your mind can't rest because you are helpless to change anything. It isn't for a lack of trying. It is simply too much. Be saved, walk with me. One more step."

"It is hard. I am not able to give anything anymore. I can't even stand up. I can't even rest. I just want to be normal again. I want to feel whole."

"Those days are behind you. You have many years of wishing for the pain to stop ahead of you. You have many years of restless misery in front of you. Those closest to you will feel the brunt of it. Eventually you will lash out at them. You will become jealous, envious, and bitter. Please, my friend, do not allow yourself to become what this world will turn you into. You are better than that. You don't deserve that, nobody does. Those close to you have hope; they have a chance to have amazing lives. They can't if you are burdening them with the cross you will need to bear. Come with me, my friend. Unburden the ones you love. They will understand in time; they will move on and they will thrive in their lives; one more step, my friend."

"My friends, my family, my work. I want to leave a legacy of kindness. I need to leave behind my stories; people can learn from them."

"Wickedness overcomes the idea of kindness all the time. There is no legacy for you, only pain and exhaustion. The legacy will be one of bitterness and pain. This is the legacy you want facing those you love? My friend, please don't do that to them. Your mark has been left; it is time for you to feel good again. Perfection is what you have earned, walk with me. See everything for the beauty it is meant to be. Let the morbidity of humankind fall away, leave it behind. It will only cause more pain and suffering to you and those you love. My friend, be at peace with just one more step."

"I try to do the right thing. I have always just wanted to be a good person. It is so hard to feel right though, it hurts so much. The nightmares get worse and worse. I dread falling asleep because of what I might hear or see. Why can't I just be at peace?"

"You may be at peace. You can't do that here though. Look at yourself, you are withering away. You are a shell of yourself. There is no coming back from where you are. Your mind, your body, these things do not fix themselves. You have done the right thing all your life, why stop now? Please, my friend, do the right thing, come with me, one more step."

The dark, angelic figure stood beside me; reaching out, it touched me. My chronic joint pain instantly melted away, the stress was lifted. At that moment, I couldn't remember ever feeling better in every conceivable way. The feeling was miraculous. I felt a healthy energy swarm over me, and I felt like a new person. As the dark angel slowly backed away, the pain returned tenfold, the trepidation flooded my mind, and the chaos my mind had been in for so long was running like a freight train. The soothing voice reached out for me to grab hold.

"One step, my brother, just one step."

The chill in the air was unrelenting; there was silence all around. There was a level of comfort and warmth coming from the angel. Though it was dark, this angel's voice was the most soothing thing I had ever heard or felt. The angel was right; to burden those closest to me with the mess I had become would be cruel. One step forward as the dark angel greeted me with love; there was a small drop from where I stood and a sudden stop. There should have been pain, but there was relief and it felt incredible; I was light-headed, I saw the smile of evil. I could no longer breathe; there was no saving me. The truth had been told and it was too late. The angel had successfully collected another soul. I was swinging slowly, unable to kick my legs as I hung. Darkness claimed its victory as it won the psychological war that had been going on for years.

Tears flowed down my face; my breath still eluded me as I shot up and out of my bed. I struggled and fought for breath—sweet air that had been removed with one step in another vivid nightmare. I didn't know what was happening to me, and I felt like I was losing my mind. The air slowly came back as the pain subsided and the tears began to flow even more steadily. I was on my knees thanking everything holy that it had just been a dream.

After a few more minutes, I had gathered myself enough to be coherent. I noticed I had many messages on my phone. As I checked my phone, I was greeted by my friend Marvin.

IT HAPPENED AGAIN, I GOT SCRATCHED, AND I FOUND THEM WHEN I WOKE UP AT 3:33 AGAIN THIS MORNING. LOOKING FORWARD TO SEEING YOU AGAIN. I DON'T KNOW WHAT IS HAPPENING DOWN HERE, BUT IT HAS BEEN ACTIVE. I read the text message.

At that moment, I understood more than ever that my chosen lifestyle would likely be the end of me. I had known all along there would undoubtedly be side effects, there would be scars, and there would be pain. My desire to tell stories and work with people would eventually lead to my death. I asked whether anybody that spent any time out of their league had ever succeeded in what they did. I asked whether or not my love and faith in a much higher and stronger power than I could understand would help me in my time of crisis. I asked if I needed to take the horrific dreams as warnings to walk away in hopes of salvaging my sanity. There were a million questions I was asking in my mind, so I began to write. I had a mountain of data to review that had been collected in Oklahoma. I knew there could be answers within, so I went back to work. I found peace and love with my work, my family, and my friends. I needed to follow my heart and my faith, and I needed to follow my love of what I was doing to see where it took me.

As I reluctantly closed my eyes, not knowing what awaited me, I fell into a deep and peaceful slumber that lasted for what felt like days. When I awoke, I felt refreshed and rejuvenated. I was ready to continue our quest. I had been given many reasons to quit, to walk away, if not run. So we faced what lay ahead with love in our hearts for the past, the present, and one another.

TWENTY-SIX

Back on the Road

JARED, RON, AND I hit the road early on that Saturday morning. There were a few things I really felt needed to get done, and we could use as much daylight as we could get. It had been quite a while since anyone had spent any time on the land, so nobody really knew what to expect, other than knowing that just about anything would be possible.

Jason Roberts and Leonard had been in regular contact with me and were both really excited for the trip. It was up in the air as to whether or not Jeremiah would make it. Jason and Leonard would be bringing a few friends with them, so there would be a decent amount of people there, and we had planned on setting up as much equipment as we could.

Marvin explained to me that they had been cleaning up Gerald's house and getting rid of a lot of the stuff that had accumulated over the years. He let me know that the house seemed to react on occasion and some strange things had been happening. They had been hearing voices and seeing doors shut on their own. Marvin's wife had also mentioned that when she was in there alone one day, out of nowhere she heard a couple claps very clearly. She felt like something was trying to get her attention. They wanted us to check out the house to see if anything happened. We had never brought in equipment and investigated that house because Gerald always seemed reluctant about it. I didn't know if it was because he was worried about the state of the house or if he was more worried about us stirring something up. Either way, I couldn't blame him.

I spoke to Annette prior to the trip and, as always, she was very excited to see everybody. Per usual, she let me know she would be making chili for everyone. One of my favorite things about going down there was being able to just sit and eat together and catch up. In many ways it felt like we were putting a family reunion together.

In the few days leading up to the trip, the nightmares had returned with a vengeance. It didn't seem to matter if it was day or night; the feeling of being stalked was always present. On the morning we hit the road for our trip, I once again felt like something heavy was nearby.

Tahlequah had been hit with a lot of rain in the days leading up to the trip, so we were greeted by a muddy mess when we arrived. The large circle driveway was a mud pit, so it was difficult to navigate our way to Gerald's house. We determined his house would be a good spot to set everything up for the night because the house had power.

"Holy shit, not again," Jared looked at me as we both laughed.

"Well buddy, did you bring your waders?" I joked.

With a sigh, Jared got out of the car and guided me down the driveway through and around the puddles. In my mind I could only think about the last time I had been down there during a storm. Jared successfully taxied the car down the driveway and we were able to park. The moment I got out of the car, the feeling of being home mixed with trepidation.

Jason Roberts and Leonard arrived right as we did, so the crew was present within minutes of our arrival. Ron, Jared, and I walked into Gerald's house and we were greeted by Marvin, Annette, and Marvin's wife. We sat down to catch up for a few minutes.

"It's pretty quiet around here, actually," Marvin told me.

"Yeah, I felt a little strange a few minutes ago, but it does feel a little different I guess," I said. My attention was turned to the china cabinet I had seen a long time ago while visiting with Gerald. I noticed the collection of kachinas was gone.

I felt let down; the discussion Gerald and I had about the kachinas awhile back had me very curious to use them as part of the investigation for the evening.

As I looked for any remains that might be useful, I felt disturbed by the fact that they were gone. I looked over toward the front door in frustration, and noticed something strange on the door. I approached it and began taking pictures. There were markings in another language that ran across the door. The markings looked similar to Arabic letters I had been familiar with. I knew they weren't in Arabic, but they were very artistic, so that is what they reminded me of.

"What the hell is this?" I said in no particular direction, "We need to get this translated."

"Whoa, that is creepy, dude," Jared said.

Our interest peaked at that moment, and we knew it could be a chore to translate the markings without some help. We documented everything as best we could and knew it was something we would have to look into. I made my way down the hallway with Marvin. He wanted to show me the other rooms in the back of the house, one of which had been blocked off for years while Gerald was still living in the home.

We entered the room at the end of the hallway and saw many shelves filled with books and trinkets. I looked through the rows of books to see if anything stood out.

"Most of this is junk I think; we just haven't cleared it all out yet. Who knows what he has hiding in here," Marvin told me.

The pressure began building in my ears before we even got to the room, but as I walked around the room, the pressure became intense. My attention was brought to the closet in the room, but I wasn't sure why. As I opened the door, I noticed some traditional Native American clothes hanging in the closet. They looked to be ceremonial.

"Go back, Brandon, go." [EVP]

"Um, dude, what the hell is that?" I said.

As I bent over, the pressure in my head felt overwhelming. For a moment I felt like my eyes might pop out of my head. I picked up the red voodoo doll that I noticed underneath some junk on the floor of the closet.

"Should you be touching that?" Jared asked as he pointed a camera at me and my newfound friend.

"I have no idea. Probably not," I said.

Marvin had burned the voodoo kit he and his wife had found when they were cleaning the place up prior to our visit. It had become very apparent they didn't find everything.

As I slowly set the doll back down on the floor of the closet, I placed a recorder in its lap. I was almost done setting it up when suddenly my hand burned as though I touched a hot stove.

"Ah, damn it, the freaking thing is hot!" I jumped back. I reached back down to confirm what my hand had felt. I touched it again, and that time I did not feel the same burn. When I raised my hand up, it looked red as though my hand was sunburned.

The sound of several people laughing was picked up on the recorder. [EVP]

"I want to use that as a trigger object tonight. We need to see if anything is attached to it," I noted.

The red doll, featuring a Mohawk of black dreadlocks and stitching for a mouth and eyes, seemed to be staring at me. I noticed there was a slice in the back of the doll—it was not on one of the seams; it appeared to have been intentional. The doll and I were fixated on each other for several minutes. I had a sudden urge to pick it up again, so I carefully set the recorder to the side and picked it up again. I ran my hand over its head to see if anything else stood out, and my finger hit a bump underneath one of the dreadlocks.

I pointed out the pin that was pushed deep into the head of the doll. I set the doll back up in the closet and placed the recorder on its lap and decided to take a breath outside. I felt like my head could explode with the amount of pressure that had built up.

I had never been in contact with a genuine doll used for ritualistic purposes. I never tied voodoo to Native American culture prior to my time in Oklahoma. All my life I thought of that as something buried in the deepest southern reaches of the country, but there could be some form of similar magic in the Native culture. The culture we had all dove headlong into was steeped in mystery and magic. Having been educated to the different types of medicine and spiritual development that had been practiced for thousands of years, it hadn't come as a complete shock to find magical ties to it.

I knew Marvin was going to ask me about getting rid of it, and I knew the doll had to be gone. I wasn't sure about the best way to dispose of something like that, so I reached out in a few different directions to see what I could find out. For that night, the doll would take the place of the kachina dolls. I didn't know if it was a good idea to go any deeper, but that night was about finding answers. There had to be some explanation for the mystery the entire area had been blanketed in.

Jared and I got into the car and headed toward the hospital to see Gerald. I was not sure how to approach a dying friend of mine in order to ask him about his deepest, darkest secrets. We drove toward the hospital and discussed the doll and wondered how it had been used. There was an undeniable energy with it, and I doubted it was the good kind of energy. We wondered out loud if even touching the thing was a mistake.

We pulled up to the hospital, parked, and went inside.

Visit with Gerald

"Help me! Please mister, help me! It hurts, please help!" A voice rang out as Jared and I slowly made our way down the halls of the hospital.

We tried to flag down an orderly to see if they could help the poor lady that was sitting in her wheelchair begging for mercy. The cries for help were disturbing. The hospital housed the sick, both mentally and physically, and the dying. We wandered the halls looking for Gerald's room; the agony in the air was brutal. There were reminders all over the place that the world could be a very cruel and lonely place.

Gerald's room was at the end of the hallway. I knocked on the door and we entered.

"Gerald, buddy? You in here?" I asked.

"Hello?" A voice came from the bathroom.

Gerald came out of the bathroom; he looked scrawny and malnourished. We embraced in a hug and he smiled as he looked at us. He slowly made his way to his bed and got comfortable. After Gerald filled us in on the hell he had been through over the past year, we discussed all our thoughts and experiences over the years.

"I was on my deathbed. I thought it was over. I was and am ready, but something won't let me go. I recovered enough to be in pain and to be reminded of all my mistakes and sins throughout my life. I am being punished. I have grown very close to God and I pray a lot, but a lot of times, the pain just reminds me of a lot of negative stuff," Gerald explained.

"I'm sorry, brother. I wish there was something I could do to help you," I said.

"I don't know how long I have; I wish I could go home with you guys because there are a lot of things I would like to show you. There are things buried on the property that I would like to dig up. Over the years, I was involved in a lot of different things and I have no doubt that a lot of it led to things being so scary on the property," he explained. "You see, years ago, I was so afraid of the things that were all around that I felt like I needed protection. Mark helped me conjure a protector, but in a lot of ways, I feel like it may have backfired. Any time you are dealing with voodoo and magic, there is a price to pay for your involvement, particularly when you use it to your benefit."

"I found the voodoo doll in your closet. Why didn't you tell me about it? Is this the type of thing that made you keep us away from your house all these years?" I asked.

"Yeah, I didn't want you getting too close to those things. Mark picked up the kachina collection, didn't he?" he asked me.

"They are all gone," I said.

"Those things are powerful. They are his, so I figured he had come to get them. Mark and I had been translating a Book of the Dead and things got really bad. I have no doubt it has something to do with me dying and dying slowly," Gerald told us.

"Jesus, Gerald, so you were living in a place where you conducted voodoo rituals, there were magic kachina dolls, and a Book of the Dead being translated?" I was floored. Everything was beginning to make sense. Mysteries were beginning to reveal themselves for what they truly were.

"I've always dabbled in different things—it isn't something I am really proud of because I do love God and I love my religion; it was just something I was very interested in and believed a lot of it could help protect me while I was out there all alone," he told us.

"*Shhhhh,*" a voice came over the recorder as I recorded our conversation.

The Book of the Dead, an ancient Egyptian text, was said to be made up of very powerful magical spells and practices. Mark and Gerald spent time together translating it from the

Sumerian language to English. As they progressed, he said things were feeling more and more dangerous all around him. I had never spoken to anyone that had admittedly involved themselves with a *Book of the Dead*. I had never seen one, though I had read about them. From what I knew, they were one of the most spiritually dangerous items in existence.

"Were you trying to hurt others with all these practices? It seems like a *Book of the Dead*, voodoo, and conjuring demons is a little bit of overkill just because you're scared. If you are scared, what in the hell makes sense about handling some of the most frightening and powerful shit known to man?" I asked.

"Some explanations go beyond words, Brandon. There are a lot of things I didn't want y'all getting too deep into down here. I didn't want you to find yourself involved in anything that could have long-term consequences. Things got really bad, so we bound the Book of the Dead. It should still be in my room. If you find it, don't unbind it, whatever you do," he said.

Gerald gave me a description of the book and I wanted badly to go back to the house that very second to look for it. I sent Jason a text asking him about it. Despite moving to Texas, he and I spoke regularly and kept in touch throughout our investigations.

STAY AWAY FROM IT. DON'T TOUCH IT. NOTHING. JUST STAY AWAY FROM IT, Jason told me bluntly.

Gerald was getting very weak and tired. He had explained he would still like to get back to the property before it was too late so he could tie up his loose ends. It was clear at that point that Gerald may have been determined to take some of his secrets with him to the grave. I felt like I couldn't force him to open up completely. Years before I had promised him that I would never force them to talk about or do anything they weren't comfortable with. I felt at that moment that Gerald needed to think on everything before filling me in with more details.

"I love you all very much. Please be careful," Gerald said as he gave me a hug.

As we drove back toward the house, Jared and I agreed there were a lot of missing pieces to the overall puzzle. We couldn't help but feel like a few of them had just been found.

TWENTY-SEVEN

Looking for Answers

WE ARRIVED BACK AT the house and trudged our way through the mud and found a place to park. We noticed another vehicle had arrived. As we walked into the house, we could smell dinner.

"Holy shit, you made it!" I greeted Jeremiah.

Jeremiah had been filled in on everything that happened prior to his arrival as we filled our bellies with delicious chili. We all talked and laughed. Everyone was in high spirits and felt like it was a night full of opportunity.

They explained to me that they kept hearing dragging noises coming from down the hallway in the house while they were setting everything up. Jason Roberts, Leonard, and their crew had set up a command center, and they had run several cameras all over the property.

Some of the crew had spent time in the old house that had provided so much activity in the past. A good portion of the ceilings had fallen down, and the floors had warped even more since our previous trips. It felt more like a death trap than ever.

After dinner, people spread out all over the property. We wanted to make sure we kept the groups small, and that we covered as much ground as we could. We had several walkie-talkies on hand to make sure we could communicate with one another while we were so spread out. The land was such a muddy mess that walking on the grass felt like walking through a swamp. Ron and I mocked one of the guys who got their truck stuck in the mud—we were each given a middle finger. Jared went back inside to finish his chili before it was time we all got to work.

"Welcome," [EVP] a voice whispered.

"Can you tell me your purpose? Do you have a job here?" I began asking questions as my eyes fixated on the little red doll sitting on the floor of the closet.

Ron, Jared, and I stood still for several minutes as we took turns asking questions. There was a stillness in the room, almost as though it was too quiet. I spent several minutes looking where Gerald said he may have hidden the Book of the Dead, but I couldn't find anything that resembled what he had described.

"So are you familiar with this Book of the Dead? Where is it?" I asked.

"Don't touch it," [EVP] another whisper was captured on the recorder sitting on the doll's lap in the closet.

"I keep hearing something; are you guys hearing something? It's like a whisper, but I can't put my finger on it," I said. I was listening to everything on a couple second delay with the RT-EVP.

"No, not hearing anything, my head kind of hurts though," Jared said.

"I thought I heard something scratching around back there," Ron said, pointing to the back of the room.

The darkness was still in the room. Jared let us know that he was getting a bad headache all of a sudden, so he went outside as Ron and I kept our line of questioning going for several more minutes.

"Uh—I just—yeah, I just felt something touching my shoulder," Ron said.

"Yeah? Nothing hanging over your shoulders or anything?" I asked.

"Nah, nothing even close. That was weird, like something put its hand on my shoulder," he finished.

I could feel the pressure in my ears; it had come and gone since we arrived earlier in the evening. The moment Ron mentioned feeling like it had touched him, I could feel the pressure build up immediately. I noted how strange it was that I felt the sensation either just before something happened or just as it was happening.

"Do you have anything to do with the feeling I get in my ears? What about Ron, did you touch Ron?" I asked.

"Don't touch, you should go." [RT-EVP]

"What was that? Did you say you touched Ron? You want us to leave?" I asked after hearing the whispery voice in my ear, "Dude, I just heard a response through the RT, pretty sure it said something about touching and wanting us to leave," I informed Ron.

We weren't getting any more responses; the pressure had gone down in my head, so we decided to head out and check on Jared. We left a recorder running in the room as we closed the door behind us and left.

Thump! A dragging noise followed the loud thump from the room we had just left.

"Did you hear that?" I asked Ron.

I quickly went back down the hallway and opened up the door to the room. Everything seemed still. "What just happened?" I asked.

Chuckling came through the headphones from the room.

"Please talk to the recorder that is in there—there's a camera in there too. You can feel free to knock it over," I said.

There weren't any more obvious sounds going on, so I went ahead and joined Jared and Ron outside.

"You feel okay, bro?" I asked Jared.

"Yeah, right when I got out here I felt like it never happened. I'm good, just needed some air I think," he said.

Ron had told Jared about the thumping sound we heard as we were headed outside. I checked in with Jeremiah, Jason, and Leonard to see if they had anything going on down in the other house or in the woods. They reported back that not much was going on other than hearing some noises in the woods as usual.

Marvin and Annette joined the three of us as we went back into the house to pull up a chair and see if anything else was going on.

We were in there several minutes, and all seemed quiet. During my review following the investigation, I found that there were a lot of footsteps all throughout the house while it had been left empty. There were voices whispering, but the words were difficult to make out. The house seemed to be very secretive; we had a few things we had noticed happening, but it seemed when we left that things really picked up.

"Ever since Gerald has been gone, it seems like things all over the place have calmed down. Any idea why? It wouldn't surprise me if a lot of the stuff around here had something to do with him and Mark. It's like they were their own coven or something," Marvin said.

"Yeah, there does seem to be a little different feel to the air. I still get that pressure in my head, but for some reason, it hasn't felt quite as overwhelming as it has in the past. I'm not sure if it has anything to do with them, but it seems like it is definitely possible. I hate not knowing for sure. I have a hard time assigning these things to people, but it does make sense," I said.

Twenty-Seven

After hearing Marvin, I began to think he was on to something regarding the fact that a lot of activity could have certainly been focused on or attached to Gerald. I knew I didn't understand the entire dynamic between Marvin and Gerald, but it was obvious there was a lot of unspoken angst between them. I genuinely cared about my friends down there very deeply, but I found myself trying to be careful not to assign blame to anybody. We were there to remain as unbiased as we could and try to explain what had been happening.

My phone rang—it was Mark. I stepped outside for a few minutes to speak with him. I had several questions for him, stemming mostly from the conversation we had with Gerald.

"Hey man, thanks for getting back to me. I had a few questions for you if you have a few minutes," I said.

"Yeah, you gonna be in town for a while?" he asked.

"Just for the night. You able to make it over? I'd like to get your thoughts on a few things," I said.

"I can't, I have to work tonight, and I won't get done until real late. What's up?" Mark asked.

"Well, I was going to ask you about some things. First, can you translate the markings we found on the door inside Gerald's house?" I asked.

"It's been a while. I'm not sure I remember, but it had something to do with the process we went through to try to put protection for Gerald in place inside the house. It is probably just something to seal off the house from whatever is around there," he told me.

"Okay, that makes sense. Am I accurate in thinking it is written in Sumerian?" I asked him.

"Yeah, for sure—probably Gerald's name written several times," he confirmed.

"What about the kachina dolls—those were yours, right?" I asked him.

"Yeah, I came and got them a few weeks ago. Gerald wanted me to go get them," he said.

"And those things have been used for a lot of different things over the years, as far as collecting and even sending out energy, right?" I asked him.

"Yeah, they are powerful. I have them put away though. Whatever energy may be attached to them should have come with them and I have them put up so it should be fine," Mark told me.

Hearing Mark's explanation about the kachina dolls made me wonder what exactly they had been used for between him and Gerald. Neither of them seemed to want to provide too many details. I understood the secrecy, but after several years, it was very frustrating feeling like information was still being withheld. Marvin and his wife would be the two living on the property moving forward, so I just hoped having the dolls gone might help in some fashion.

"What do you know about the voodoo doll we found in the closet?" I asked him.

"It has been used, it's authentic. I can't really talk about the details. There could be bad consequences to that," he said. He sounded surprised that we had found it.

"It seems like a lot of things are involved here that aren't quite as innocent as being the victim of a haunted property. You know most of the things we are talking about can make an already haunted property very dangerous, right?" I asked.

"Right. The place has seen a lot over the generations. Not all of it is innocent—that is for sure. There is very likely a combination of different forces and energies that are there to stay; they all found their way to the property for one reason or another. It would be impossible to say exactly how and why everything came to be there," Mark told me.

"Gerald mentioned having some items buried throughout the property. Do you have any idea what those items are and why they were buried?" I asked.

"Well, he could be talking about a number of things. There have been relics buried there, specifically at the four corners of the property; they shouldn't be bothered," Mark said.

"Yeah, he mentioned the relics. Are those part of the protection process?" I followed up.

"Yes, they serve many purposes, but protection would be one," he said.

"What else might be buried there besides the relics? Are we talking about bodies?" I asked him.

"That is probably what he was talking about. There are supposedly several bodies that have been buried over the years that are in unmarked graves. Obviously, they should not be disturbed either," Mark told me.

"Right, I get that. Wondering if maybe there should be some type of marking though to at least commemorate them. Do you know where they might be?" I asked him.

"No, sorry dude, I don't. I better run. Good luck—let me know if there is anything else I can help with," Mark brought our conversation to an abrupt ending.

Immediately after getting off the phone with Mark I grabbed my dowsing rods and went outside. I had some daylight left and wanted to use them in some specific places on the property that Jason had long ago felt were significant. I felt I needed to see what the dowsing rods led me to.

There are many different types of dowsing rods, but in their most basic form, they are two "L" shaped rods made out of some type of metal or even twigs. Sometimes the rods can be in a "Y" shape, but I have always used the "L" shaped rods. As the investigator holds a rod in each hand, they are held loosely to allow the rods to guide you. There is a plastic casing around the short end of the "L" shape and a small ball on each end of the long side of the rods, which provides some weight, so when the rod pulls in one direction or another, the feeling is very obvious. With the plastic casing, the rods can swing freely in one direction or the other without the investigator worrying about holding the rods too tightly. What the investigator is looking for is to have the rods cross one another naturally without assisting them. When they cross, there is an almost magnetic pull that the investigator can feel and that spot could potentially be a place of interest.

I made my way to the backyard of the old, abandoned house and walked toward the back corner that Jason had once pointed out. Jason had strong feelings that there were unmarked graves in close proximity to the abandoned house, so I was determined to find the spots if at all possible. I trudged through the mud and walked on the soft ground making my way back there; when I arrived, I stopped and just looked around. Before I had even made it all the way to the back area, I felt like I was being watched.

I began slowly walking back and forth throughout the yard area that bordered the woods. I made my way back and forth, allowing the rods to freely swing in any direction. The spongy ground felt as though it might swallow me at any moment; I kept moving. The feeling of being watched was getting stronger and stronger the longer I was back there. I kept hearing the angry voice from the first night we investigated this place saying "Look in back." I felt more and more certain that something significant was back there.

I had covered almost every foot of the backyard area and had very little in the way of guidance from my dowsing rods. They simply swung back and forth. I hadn't felt any kind of pull in any direction. I was walking around the edge of the woods when suddenly both rods pointed to my left. As I turned slowly in the direction they were pointing, they straightened out. Finally, I was being guided in a specific direction—at least

I hoped so. There was a slight opening in the thick woods. I slowly stepped into the woods and could still feel the magnetism coming from the rods, so I slowly moved forward. To test the situation, I turned every few feet in one direction or the other to see if the rods would pull me back, and they did. I was walking in a westerly direction from the house as the sun was beginning to sink behind the horizon. When I got about fifty yards from the entrance of the woods, the rods crossed. For the first time since I began my walk, the K-II meter I had in the kangaroo pouch of my hooded sweatshirt also lit up. I paused, grabbed the handheld GPS out of my backpack, and marked the spot where I was standing. I knew the GPS would only be accurate within a certain radius, but at that point, I just needed to make sure I could mark the location. I kept walking slowly around the area to see if I could find any other location that might stand out. The rods wanted to point back to the spot I had already marked until I got about six feet or so to the other side, and they crossed again.

"Is this where I need to be?" I asked as my body and mind began to feel paranoid. There was nobody anywhere near me at the time, but I could feel eyes all around me.

I heard a familiar grumbling behind me as I turned around as quickly as I could, only to find nothing standing there.

"Release me," a childlike voice whispered into the recorder.

The growling persisted every few seconds; it seemed to come from different directions each time. As I stood speechless in the woods, I felt sick. I felt like I was surrounded by sadness and sickness. My nightmares came flooding over me. It was as though I was standing in broad daylight in the middle of one of the death camps I had dreamt about. I couldn't tell if I was trespassing on holy or cursed ground. I found myself dropped to my knees in the middle of the woods and saying a prayer. I prayed that anything holy would comfort the lost souls that might be stuck on the property. I said the Hail Mary and Our Father; I didn't know what else to do. I was overcome with so many emotions.

"You can rest—if you see a light, go toward it. You can be at peace," I said, choking back tears.

The K-II meter reacted as I knelt on the ground. My body hurt and my mind felt like it was melting, but I knew something needed to be said. The growling had subsided, but the feeling of being watched and completely overwhelmed had gotten stronger. I felt like I had slept as I slowly got to my feet. It was as though much time had lapsed while I began to wander back toward the houses. I could hear rustling in the leaves, but when I looked around, I could not see anything.

I got back to the group just before dark. Jared came over to me to make sure I was all right. I reassured him that I was good, although something still felt very uncomfortable. Without having my brother and Jason there, I felt a little lost. Jared gave me a swift reminder that I wasn't alone. He had been by my side the entire time; knowing that allowed me to get myself centered and back to work.

Everyone had been spread out all over the property for a few hours. Nobody had reported anything too perplexing, other than a few unexplained noises and some odd feelings.

Jared, Ron, and I had spent most of the evening in Gerald's house since we never had the chance to investigate it. The markings all over the house, the mysterious Book of the Dead, and our little red friend in the closet had piqued my interest. There wasn't much going on other than some strange reactions from the equipment.

The hours ticked by and nobody had anything outrageous to report. We all gathered together in Gerald's house and I let everyone know the Kansas City crew was going to have to call it a night. There was a very long drive ahead of us, so we needed to hit the road. Our friends from Wichita went back to their camp to make sure everything was good for the night.

Marvin and I sat down to talk about the night.

"Not much going on tonight—there is a different feeling overall down here right now. I can admit that I'm not sure what to make of it. I know you said since Gerald has been gone things feel different; I don't know how to explain that, but if you have experienced this since he has been gone, then you would know better than me," I told him.

"Yeah, it has been a lot different since he's been gone. I think things have calmed down a lot. There are still things going on here and there, but overall, it ain't as bad as it was. My wife has had some experiences, but I wonder if that damn doll in there and all this crap on the walls has anything to do with all that," he replied.

We spoke for a long time about how he was wanting to re-establish residence on the property, but he wanted to make sure it was safe.

"I don't know what to tell you, brother. This place has blown my mind more times than I can count. Things have happened down here that I never thought even remotely possible. I can tell you for sure that this place has affected me even after I leave. I will always want to learn more about this place and see what else it has to offer. It is remarkable. I need to figure out the best way to get rid of that damn doll though. I don't have a lot of experience with that, so I need to look into it," I said.

"I was gonna just burn it. You think that would be bad?" Marvin asked.

"I don't know. I'm looking into it right now. We'll figure it out. One thing is for sure though; you need to get in touch with whomever you need to get in touch with about getting this whole property cleansed. I know I probably can't be involved with whatever they do, but it needs to be done. I don't know if you are ever going to have a piece of property that doesn't have something strange going on, but I can imagine it being livable," I told him.

"A lot of stuff has happened here over a lot of years," Marvin said. "I know people have done stuff to bring more here than what was already here. It pisses me off, but that is what happened. I want to be here, so we are going to try. I guess we grew up different than most. We just lived with all of it. It was scary, and it still is sometimes, but it was just us. It was our life; there is a spiritual thing that is in certain cultures that maybe draws this stuff in sometimes. Shit—aliens, monsters, ghosts, demons—all of it. This has been our home for a long time, but our ancestors didn't choose to leave their homes to walk here," he explained.

As we discussed the past for a little while, I felt like Marvin had accepted many of the things that happened in his life and gained a peace within himself. He seemed like a different person as we sat and talked. He had always been very interested in being involved with the process of investigating and looking for answers. Not many people experience the type of reality we had all experienced over the course of several years. The area we investigated was magical; the world went on outside its walls, but those that experienced it got a glimpse behind the flimsy veil of what exists just beyond our minds.

"It looks like you can burn that doll, but you'll want to take it off the property first," I told him after hearing back from a couple different sources.

"Good, I want to get rid of that thing. We just want to make sure we can do whatever we can to have this place work out for a while. It has been in the family for so long. I want to farm it and make it livable. I'll get in touch with the Cherokee Nation to see what they can do about helping with a blessing and cleansing on the property. I would like for you to be here, but I know a lot of that stuff they want to keep in the community. They don't broadcast a lot of that kind of thing, but if you think it will help, I will make some calls," he told me.

"I think that is a good plan. I don't know about the markings on the door. I think we have translated at least some of it. Jeremiah and I have looked in several different directions and the markings appear to be either Sumerian or something called Theban. Sumerian is common for a lot of things that are used in different types of ritualistic activity. Theban is usually known to be tied to the Wiccan religion and can oftentimes be used for some sort of conjuring as well. I asked Jason about it; he does believe at least part of it calls out something demonic. Nothing is marked with a demonic name that has intention of keeping it away. That isn't the way it works. The names aren't something that should really be said out loud, let alone scripted on walls and doors within a home—especially if the intention is to keep it out," I explained.

"That is crazy, yeah; I want all this stuff to go away. Do you think him being gone has anything to do with the fact that things have calmed down?" Marvin asked.

"I think only time can answer that question. There does seem to be a different feel around here than what we are used to, but saying for sure that it is directly tied to Gerald might be a bit presumptuous. I don't think it will be possible to pinpoint the genesis of all the activity, but I do believe that he may have contributed to at least some of it. I also believe a lot of it is attached to the land. A lot of these things date back thousands of years—as old as humanity. This land has seen a lot of tragedy over many generations; it has also seen a lot of interaction with unknown forces. Conjuring something could add to or open up already existing scars within the land. I think a lot of the things you guys have experienced in your lives may stem from the magic and medicine that was practiced by a lot of the elders. I think it is pretty clear that a lot of the feuding between families contributed to a lot of the attacks that have taken place over the years. There have been countless sightings of ghosts and creatures, at least one suicide on the property, and likely several unmarked graves. All those things put together could potentially lead to all sorts of unexplainable activity," I told Marvin, attempting to give him my feelings and interpretation.

"A lot of the research I have done that initially led me here has to do with geographic locations and their significance. I believe there are locations all over the world that act as conductors of earth energy and can be potential hot spots of paranormal activity. In my opinion, a true holocaust happened to your people during the Trail of Tears. Your people were led here under unspeakable conditions from their homes, and it all stopped right here in this area. That energy and sadness came with them. I was looking at my ley line map, and the number of intersecting lines within the region is staggering. What was also very interesting was the fact that the path of one of the main highways used during the Trail of Tears follows almost exactly one of the ley lines that intersects with several others here. It looks as though the people that moved the Cherokee knew about this highway of energy and followed it all the way here."

"Wow, I never thought about any of that. When the people got here, they tried to reestablish their way of life, but the bitterness never really faded. It was swept under the rug by everybody, and I think that has been a reason a lot of the hatred between families and between the white folk and Cherokee has stuck around for so long," Marvin said.

"Yeah, well, I have looked into both the Trail of Tears and what is known as the Holocaust that took place in Europe during World War II, and the similarities are uncanny. It was as though history attempted to repeat itself in the 1940s. Ironically, the US stepped in and helped put an end to that travesty, but it was nearly too late. Unfortunately, there was nobody to step in to defend the Natives during the Trail of Tears. The true founding fathers and mothers of this land were at the mercy of a merciless regime that saw nothing but dollar signs and an opening to take control. These crimes against humanity are unforgivable, and the government has found it much easier to squash the details and keep them from the mainstream education system. So many times I have been here with you, my friends, and felt the need to say I am sorry for the past," I told Marvin.

Marvin and I spoke for a little while longer. We both felt like certain details had come to light that might truly lead to a better life on the land. Until that night, we had not known the facts about what had gone on for many years behind closed doors all over the area. It was impossible to say to what extent the land had been marred by lashing out by the inhabitants.

All we could do was focus on the place Marvin and his wife would hopefully call home for many years to come.

"We have been at this for over four years, and I believe we have all learned more about what is and is not possible than most people will in a lifetime. I also wanted to tell you—every time I stand at the other end of the driveway near the fire pit and look out across the field to the north, I still feel like that could have been some type of battleground at some point. You said there have been countless artifacts found in and around the area, like arrowheads and even bones. Being on a hill, I feel like there is a very good possibility that the bodies buried on or near this property may stretch well beyond the handful that are thought to be close by in unmarked graves. In my opinion, there is a very good chance that this place may be unsettled by the fact that it could be a significant burial ground. There have been recent discoveries that indicate many Native tribes inhabited these lands long before the establishment of even what are now known as Native American tribes. There are findings being unearthed almost every day that date back well beyond documented civilizations that existed here," I said, attempting to bring a perspective into the conversation. I hoped Marvin could look deeper than what may have been handed down as stories from his ancestors.

"That makes sense. It is amazing to think that far back and wonder what may have happened all over the place. We just think about the way things look now," he said.

"Things happened all around us that we have no idea about. Those things are just as significant as what was documented. Some pasts are more tragic than others, but I think one would be hard-pressed to take a step anywhere in this country that has not at some point seen some sort of tragedy. If you believe this stuff exists, it doesn't have to simply exist where a murder or battle took place. It doesn't have to be confined within the walls of a hospital that breathes death or a prison that breathes despair. Of course those places can be super-charged with frightening energy, but to not think beyond those walls would be irresponsible of me as an investigator. There are stories to be told all over the country, and your home has provided an amazing story," I told Marvin as he nodded in agreement.

"I'll see what I can do about getting someone here to give this place some peace. If I can have you down, I will let you know. I'll talk to them about that doll, too. They may want to take it with them and dispose of it," Marvin said.

"I would love to be here and go through the cleansing process. I think it would be therapeutic for all of us in many ways, but the land is what needs peace. There are so many spirits wandering around that I think something like that could help so many. I do believe there are dark forces here that cause fear and even affect those that have passed on. The soldiers of Satan are everywhere. They aren't always making noises or moving objects; sometimes they focus on the psychological side of things. They can also collect and trap souls, which I believe may have happened here. Just remember, Satan's greatest trick was convincing many he doesn't exist. I believe that something as old as time and as powerful as many of these forces can easily work its way into our minds and do the most damage.

"If you think about it, if they can make someone appear to others to lose their minds and then be called crazy, they have complete control over the mind and body of that person. Talk about a helpless situation. Something that strong simply takes ownership of a person; I can't think of many things more frightening than that," I said.

"I never really thought of it like that. I've heard stories of people getting possessed—I've even seen someone change right in front of me," Marvin added.

"We have both had dreams and physical issues that have come up that show maybe we are too close or even marked by something that can be really dangerous. All we can really do is keep our faith in the good side of things and rely on each other to understand where we are coming from. I think I have things following me around all the time; maybe one day something will strike. I try to do the best I can to protect my family, friends, and myself from being affected by the things I have encountered. Investigating is something I feel like I am meant to do. I feel like I was meant to meet and become friends with you and Annette and Gerald," I said.

"Well, don't you be a stranger. Even if things calm down, y'all are always welcome down here. You know that.

I want you to be here for the cleansing. You have saved our lives on a lot of levels. Before y'all started coming down, I didn't understand any of this. Since you have, I have gained strength and I have had you there to help me believe it's possible to be safe. I know I will deal with these things for the rest of my life, but I truly believe we can limit the extent and live peacefully. There ain't any perfect place or perfect life, but we can do the best we can to be happy here. I wouldn't have believed that was possible until I got a chance to work with y'all. I thank all of you," Marvin said.

Ron, Jared, and I made our way over to the camp to say our goodbyes to our friends from Wichita. Not a lot had happened during the course of the investigation on that particular night, but we all knew from our experiences that the place was unlike any other we had been to. We didn't know the next time we could all sit and enjoy each other's company at a location like this, so we sat around the fire and talked about the many experiences we had. I didn't open up about my solo investigation. I didn't know if I had the ability to explain how deeply the place had dug into my soul. I kept the fact that I had seen my own face physically change before my eyes a secret. I felt in my heart there was a way for Marvin and his wife to live on the land without having to live in constant fear. I did believe that there could be things that would not go away no matter what type of cleansing might be done. My hope was to see my friends coexist with a past that could never be completely removed from their sacred land. It was the type of place that needed to be respected, not necessarily feared.

We bid farewell to our friends and began our trip home. As we drove down the dark, gravel road toward the highway, I thought back to the first time we drove away from the property. The feeling of knowing that place had hooked me like a drug was unforgettable. I couldn't stop thinking about one other experience I had—something inexplicable that I felt I needed to come face to face with.

I pulled up and parked the car near the entrance to Manus Cemetery.

"If you guys want to hang out, just give me a minute. I'll be right back," I told the guys. I got out of the car and made my way to the entrance.

I slowly made my way back to the corner of the graveyard, stepping softly on the mushy grounds. As I approached the back fence, I took a pouch out of my pocket and knelt down with my attention toward the wooded area just outside of the fence line. I set a small stuffed doll on the ground and spread some tobacco on the ground that I had brought with me.

"All I ask is that you protect the souls that have been laid to rest here. I never wanted to offend you or anything that may be here. I know you meant to contact me, and I thank you for giving me the opportunity to see something I never thought possible. I hope to come back some day, but I wanted to give you these small gifts as a sign of love and respect. My life will never be the same. You scared me, but you affected me in a spiritual way. Thank you," I said, wondering what might be near enough to hear my words.

With each step inside the fence of the cemetery, I always knew there was something or someone around. There was a quiet yet eerie peace that filled the air that night. I felt an appreciation for being able to look back on the place that had changed my perspective when I didn't think that was possible. I made my way back to the car, and we were back on the road headed home.

Conclusion

FOR OVER FOUR YEARS, many people gave their time and energy to a little-known place that had managed to resonate in their lives. A mysterious land shrouded in darkness had come like a bull and staked its claim on some portion of all our minds and souls. Throughout the world, there are places that defy logic, reason, and even science on many levels; this was one of them—a place none of us could ever forget. The word "impossible" has found nearly no place in my vocabulary since experiencing the things in Tahlequah, Oklahoma. Until locations like these have the chance to work their way into a person's soul, there are no words to give justice to what is truly possible in the world we all call home. This place may have been covered in darkness on so many levels, but it also exuded a peaceful calm—further proof that there may be darkness all around, but there is also light.

Years had gone by and the tone of despair and helplessness I had found within the eyes of this second family had been replaced with hope and strength. Generations of tales and experiences had given us all reason to wonder if the land had truly been cursed for eternity. With our latest meeting, everyone walked away believing there might always be something mysterious and even frightening lurking in the shadows of the land, but we believed with all our hearts that there was a chance the land and its inhabitants could find some peace.

My phone rang. My very good friend needed to fill me in.

"So about an hour after you guys left, we noticed one of the cameras went out," Jeremiah said.

"Yeah? That's weird," I replied.

"Well, the strange thing was, it was well after everyone but us had gone for the night. We were still wandering around in different places and Jason noticed the camera had gone out, so we went to take a look. Turns out the cable connected to the camera looked like it had been cut. It wasn't chewed through or anything. It looked like someone had some sharp scissors and just cut right through it. It was really weird," he told me.

"What the hell, dude! It was just cut? Have you been able to review the camera footage to see if you could hear or see anything leading up to when it went out?" I asked him.

"Yeah, we couldn't hear shit. There could have been some rustling or something, but it was so subtle, it would be impossible to say. But the cable was cut about a foot or so below the camera itself, so it wasn't laying on the ground or anything. When we found that, we didn't know if we could say for sure that we were actually alone on the property. We hung out for a little while and finished up, but we decided it may not be the best idea to stay for the night, so we packed up and took off," he said.

"That's freaking crazy, dude. I'm sorry that happened. That sucks. I guess we need to chalk that up to another mystery, huh? Like we needed more of those down there!" I told him as we both chuckled.

"Seriously, obviously we can't say it was paranormal or anything, but it was the camera that was pointing outside Gerald's house. I can't think of anything that would just slice right through it as cleanly as it did. Nobody was around though, so that was pretty creepy. We figured if someone was sneaking around out there, we didn't want to be around if they decided to come into camp or something. Thanks again for having us down, dude. What an amazing place," he said.

"Thanks for making it down. It's always our pleasure to work with you guys. I'm sorry about the cable—at least the camera wasn't broken or anything. You guys stay safe; we need to figure out a time to get together again sometime soon. I know you aren't going to be as active as you used to be, but I'm going to get in touch with you when I find the next project. I expect you to help me out," I insisted that Jeremiah never completely remove himself from the world of investigating. I understood that life happens and investigating takes more out of people than what those uninvolved could realize, but he and

I had always had great chemistry and a great working relationship. Outside of those closest to me, Jeremiah had been someone I trusted and worked easily with for several years. I would always respect his wishes, but would never promise him that I would not want his help in the future.

"For sure, bro. You let me know and I'm always happy to help in any way I can. Talk to you soon, brother. Take care of yourself," he said.

I couldn't help but spend time wondering what happened to their cable. It was impossible to know without a camera picking up the evidence, but my mind wandered in many directions. That place would not let go—that was clear. I wondered if at some point down the road, following a thorough cleansing and ridding of the things that harbor negativity, Marvin would tell me that nothing they tried did any good. It seemed like a place beyond salvation at the beginning of the process; it felt like a cesspool of negativity. By the time we drove away at the end of our most recent investigation, there was an air of hope. When Jeremiah told me about the cable, I had to wonder if something or someone was stalking the situation and sending some sort of sign or message.

The history tied to the location had broken my heart and left me wondering at what point humanity might focus on loving and embracing one another instead of fighting over things that are petty in the big picture of our collective existence. I could feel my soul weeping for those lost for eternity at the brutal hands of those in power. I could still hear the screams and moans carry through the foothills of the Ozarks as though the massacre were still happening. The sadness that floods those lands cut my soul like a knife. My best attempts to separate my personal life from my experiences were clearly futile. In the line of work I had been called to do, my personal life was also my professional life. The requirement to bring my faith and beliefs with me wherever I went would mold my life in the days and years that lie ahead.

The side effects surround me almost daily. My nightmares bring the reality of the past back to life; sometimes it feels as though the shame and guilt bestowed upon me by our ancestors would devour me. My research has taken me to many places over the years, but none of those places carried with it the burden of sadness in the same manner that Tahlequah did. This had been the first time that so many stories had been lumped together within such a small geographic area.

As time passed, the nightmares became less common. I stayed in regular contact with my friends in Oklahoma. Gerald had recovered enough from his latest bout of cancer to move into an apartment and was living on his own and doing pretty well. He and I had spoken at great length about the remaining secrets and my desire to know the truth about as much as I could. For reasons unbeknownst to me, he was insistent about keeping some details to himself. I understood, but it wasn't without frustration. My heart was joyful with the fact that he was still around and still stirring up trouble as only he could do. We spoke about faith and life. He would always ask about my family and things going on in my life. One day, his unmistakable laugh and endless curiosities would be extinguished, but it was clear that until that day came, he would continue to leave his mark on the world and those around him. Gerald has a spark within him that is extremely rare. There may be a dark side, and there may have been mistakes made in the past, but in the end he is a genuine and amazing person.

I never convinced myself that he was perfect or without flaws. None of us are, and I appreciated the fact that Gerald would always admit his flaws and simply move on knowing he was who he was and nothing would ever change that. We agreed that some of his mistakes and decisions might be things he could pay for in some way for a long time, but in the end, he owned them. He said he was content with who he was and what awaited him in the future. In many ways, I was envious of the clarity he seemed to be going through the remaining days of his life with.

I spoke to Marvin with regularity and he told me he was still working on getting the cleansing of the land organized. I made it a point to remind him how important it was. I told him if he needed me present, I would be happy to make it happen. He let me know he and his wife were continuing to work on the land and were making great progress with getting the rest of their lives set up. We didn't speak of certain things that involved him and Gerald, but he would tell me his thoughts and frustrations about everything. I simply reminded him that I cared about both of them and that would never change. I was happy that the land looked like it would stay in good and caring hands for the foreseeable future.

Marvin would always remind me that he could still feel something out of place when he was spending a lot of time on the property. He still felt himself being watched. They would still hear things moving around. I let him know we needed to see what happened after some time passed when the cleansing was done. He let me know they were going to be replacing the door that had all the markings on it. We talked about the future and we looked for opportunities to spend time together without having to worry about working.

Annette and I sent text messages to each other often. She always asked me about family and life and everything in between. I did the same with her. She is one of the kindest souls I have ever known in this lifetime. We talked about getting together in the future. Everyone had their daily lives to tend to, but we all had a bond that would not be broken with passing time.

There was no way to tell what might happen in the future. My hope was that Marvin would find assistance in bringing relief to the land he insisted on calling home.

Throughout the entire time I worked in Oklahoma, I looked at my own roots and ancestry. Beyond one relative many generations ago that was full-blooded Cherokee, I had no Native American blood running through my veins, but I did feel a kinship and connection with my friends. My mind had to wrap around things I never thought possible; I had to look at the world differently than I did before. There is always a fine line drawn in conducting investigations that required a healthy skepticism while ensuring I held an open mind no matter what I had been told. From the day we arrived in Oklahoma on that February day, reality changed on many levels for me. I could feel the history in the air; it was with us as we took each step. Stories of aliens, witches, demons, ghosts, monsters, and so much more seemed like an outlandish fictional story that had been shoved down our throats by people we did not know prior to our chance meeting. It was all impossible.

With each passing trip, impossible became more and more possible. I had to wonder if the messages sent to us stating the property was some type of purgatory was truly a description of what the place really was. The land had felt for so long that it was some type of encampment for damned souls. Before we could tell what had hit us, we found ourselves sitting and discussing how even the most outlandish claims gave us reason to doubt our initial reactions. While attempting to remain professional and unbiased, the thing that had become the most difficult was convincing ourselves that anything was truly possible. Not a day passed by that I didn't find myself thinking about Oklahoma—I felt I needed to go back. I knew the place that had transformed my life personally, spiritually, and professionally was not done with me. One day I knew there would be more truth to come out—I knew there would be more memories and trips. We would laugh and likely shed tears together as we had already. I didn't know if the spirits of the land would rear their heads again. I hoped measures would be taken that could allow for a peaceful existence for both the living and the dead.

I found myself waking up, not from a nightmare, but to a noise I couldn't make out. I wasn't sure what had woken me, but I was inclined to get out of bed to look for the source of the sound. I made my way through the house, making sure nobody was awake and moving around. It was the dead of night, not long before the sun would peek through the darkness. I went outside and began walking down the stairs from the deck to my backyard. I decided to snap some pictures in the yard. I felt something watching me. I was not sure if that feeling would ever completely go away or if it would go away at all, for that matter. I did not see or hear anything out of the ordinary, but I felt compelled to take my walk toward the nearby cemetery. I thought about watching the sunrise.

There was a low-lying fog that slowly floated across the ground as I made my way down the street. I walked through the entrance to the cemetery. The vision was both haunting and beautiful. The sunshine of the day began wrestling with the final charge of the darkness before giving way. The fog straddled the ground, and I stood in the heart of the peaceful place of rest, watching and listening. I heard a familiar sound rustling nearby, followed by a low grumbling. As I looked toward the darkest corner of the cemetery, I could see a pair of red eyes glowing as though they had just been outfitted with a new set of batteries. They didn't blink; they simply stared at me through the remaining pitch black of night. My peripheral vision saw the glow of the sun peeking over the dark horizon while my eyes fixated on the continued glow peering in my direction. I pointed my camera as a low grumble came from the source of the glow—as soon as I snapped the picture, the glow disappeared with the flash of my camera and the blink of my eyes.

I stood there wondering why I wasn't petrified. I just stood frozen and wondered if this creature was a good thing or something evil that was stalking me and biding its time before wreaking havoc on me. I felt and heard it regularly; it had desensitized me to an extent, as I no longer shivered with fear when I felt its presence. I knew one day I would find out. Until then, I would walk alone in the darkness seeking answers and hoping to bring a glimmer of light along with me.

I slowly turned toward the glow that became a bright, warm light. I sat down next to a tree that looked over the horizon, and through the surrounding wilderness I watched the birth of another day.

GET MORE AT LLEWELLYN.COM

Visit us online to browse hundreds of our books and decks, plus sign up to receive our e-newsletters and exclusive online offers.

- Free tarot readings • Spell-a-Day • Moon phases
- Recipes, spells, and tips • Blogs • Encyclopedia
- Author interviews, articles, and upcoming events

GET SOCIAL WITH LLEWELLYN

Find us on Facebook
www.Facebook.com/LlewellynBooks

Follow us on **twitter**
www.Twitter.com/Llewellynbooks

GET BOOKS AT LLEWELLYN

LLEWELLYN ORDERING INFORMATION

Order online: Visit our website at www.llewellyn.com to select your books and place an order on our secure server.

Order by phone:
- Call toll free within the U.S. at 1-877-NEW-WRLD (1-877-639-9753)
- Call toll free within Canada at 1-866-NEW-WRLD (1-866-639-9753)
- We accept VISA, MasterCard, American Express, and Discover

Order by mail:
Send the full price of your order (MN residents add 6.875% sales tax) in U.S. funds, plus postage and handling to: Llewellyn Worldwide, 2143 Wooddale Drive, Woodbury, MN 55125-2989

POSTAGE AND HANDLING:
STANDARD: (U.S. & Canada)
(Please allow 12 business days)
$30.00 and under, add $4.00.
$30.01 and over, FREE SHIPPING.

INTERNATIONAL ORDERS:
$16.00 for one book, plus $3.00 for each additional book.

Visit us online for more shipping options.
Prices subject to change.

FREE CATALOG!

To order, call
1-877-NEW-WRLD
ext. 8236
or visit our website

the house where EVIL LURKS

A PARANORMAL INVESTIGATOR'S MOST FRIGHTENING ENCOUNTER

BRANDON CALLAHAN

The House Where Evil Lurks
A Paranormal Investigator's Most Frightening Encounter
BRANDON CALLAHAN

This story gives the reader an insight into the process of investigating paranormal activity. The story allows the reader to understand that investigations are not always portrayed accurately on television.

The haunting explored in this book has major implications on a family's life as well as on the people involved in the investigation process. *The House Where Evil Lurks* shows that evil exists in the world, and it helps the reader understand that true evil operates on a physical as well as psychological level.

This book holds nothing back in showing just how devastating the potential consequences might be for anyone involving themselves in this field of research.

978-0-7387-4066-9, 264 pp., 5³⁄₁₆ x 8   **$15.99**

To order, call 1-877-NEW-WRLD
Prices subject to change without notice
Order at Llewellyn.com 24 hours a day, 7 days a week

THE UNINVITED

STEVEN LaCHANCE
with LAURA LONG-HELBIG

The True Story of the Union Screaming House

The Uninvited
The True Story of the Union Screaming House
STEVEN A. LACHANCE

What kind of evil lives at the Union Screaming House?

In this true and terrifying firsthand account, Steven LaChance reveals how he and his three children were driven from their Union, Missouri, home by demonic attackers.

LaChance chronicles how the house's relentless supernatural predators infest those around them. He consults paranormal investigators, psychics, and priests, but the demonic attacks—screams, growls, putrid odors, invisible shoves, bites, and other physical violations—only grow worse. The entities clearly demonstrate their wrath and power: killing family pets, sexually assaulting individuals, even causing two people to be institutionalized.

The demons' next target is the current homeowner, Helen. When the entities take possession and urge Helen toward murder and madness, LaChance must engage in a hair-raising battle for her soul.

978-0-7387-1357-1, 264 pp., 6 x 9   **$16.95**

To order, call 1-877-NEW-WRLD
Prices subject to change without notice
Order at Llewellyn.com 24 hours a day, 7 days a week

STEVEN A. LaCHANCE
with SHANNON N. LUSK

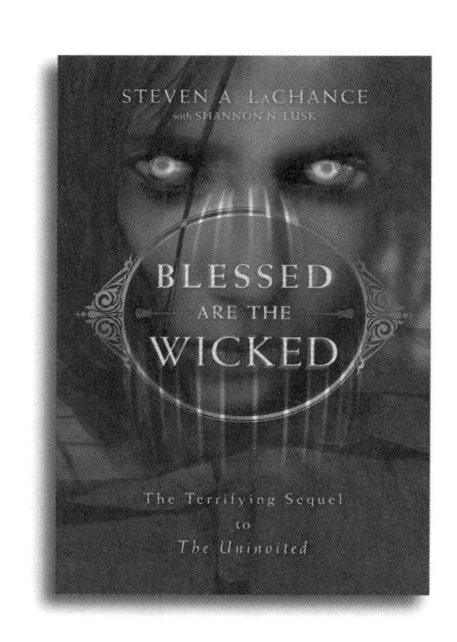

BLESSED ARE THE WICKED

The Terrifying Sequel
to
The Uninvited

Blessed Are the Wicked
The Terrifying Sequel to The Uninvited
STEVEN A. LACHANCE

Steven LaChance took us through his own personal hell in *The Uninvited*. Even though he moved out of the house, it still had a grip on him and his family. They helped the woman who currently lived in the house through the horrors of life there.

Blessed Are the Wicked is the continuation of the story. Literally fighting for his life, LaChance tells the story behind the horror of the Union house and the battle against the evil that still lies there.

978-0-7387-3896-3, 264 pp., 6 x 9   **$16.99**

To order, call 1-877-NEW-WRLD
Prices subject to change without notice
Order at Llewellyn.com 24 hours a day, 7 days a week

FIGHTING MALEVOLENT SPIRITS

SAMANTHA E. HARRIS

A DEMONOLOGIST'S DARKEST ENCOUNTERS

Fighting Malevolent Spirits
A Demonologist's Darkest Encounters
SAMANTHA E. HARRIS

A family builds a home at the site of an old sanitarium and is plunged into the depths of addiction, violence, and self harm. A demon repeatedly throws a young man across a room. Incessant knocking and ghostly shrieks of pain drive a researcher to the point of insanity.

Samantha E. Harris is a long-time demonologist and paranormal investigator. The stories collected here are her darkest, creepiest, and most terrifying cases. In *Fighting Malevolent Spirits*, she tells tales of beastly encounters with poltergeists, demons, and unhappy spirits of the dead. This book also includes a question-and-answer section to help determine the cause of a paranormal disturbance and how-to instructions for removing negative spirits.

978-0-7387-3697-6, 240 pp., 5³⁄₁₆ x 8 $14.99

To order, call 1-877-NEW-WRLD
Prices subject to change without notice
Order at Llewellyn.com 24 hours a day, 7 days a week

THE SALLIE HOUSE HAUNTING

A TRUE STORY

DEBRA PICKMAN

The Sallie House Haunting
A True Story
Debra Lyn Pickman

This is the firsthand account of what Tony and Debra Pickman and their newborn son Taylor experienced in the now notorious Sallie House, from the day they moved in to the turn-of-the-century haunted house until they finally fled in terror. The story of the Sallie House and the fire-starting ghost girl who haunted it has sparked endless rumors and theories of murder, cover-ups, racism, and abuse. But the Pickmans know the real story because they lived it—and barely made it out alive.

Now, for the first time, Tony and Debra reveal untold stories from their ordeal. They describe Sallie's seemingly protective fascination with their baby and tell what it was like to live with menacing entities that scratched, bit, and terrorized their family. Along with historical research, the Pickmans share personal photographs and journal entries from their time spent living in the nightmare house that still haunts them today.

978-0-7387-2128-6, 288 pp., 6 x 9   **$16.95**

To order, call 1-877-NEW-WRLD
Prices subject to change without notice
Order at Llewellyn.com 24 hours a day, 7 days a week

A Ghost Hunter's Most Terrifying Case...to Date
DEVIL
IN THE DELTA
RICH NEWMAN

Devil in the Delta
A Ghost Hunter's Most Terrifying Case ... to Date
RICH NEWMAN

A television that shoots fire. Objects flying through the air. A demonic possession. A ghost hunter's worst nightmare.

When author Rich Newman first arrives at the battered doublewide trailer deep in the Mississippi Delta, it's clear that this is no ordinary haunting. Called from Memphis to assist a local ghost hunting team, Newman's investigation of the Martin House has become his most terrifying and mysterious case to date.

What starts out as a malicious assault quickly spirals into a story of obsession, possession, witchcraft, and murder. When the evidence becomes overwhelming, long-buried memories from Newman's past come back to haunt him—memories he'd rather forget. Collecting physical evidence, researching the violent history of the property, and interviewing the world's most famous demonologists, Newman's investigation of the Martin House plunges him into the darkest depths of the unknown.

978-0-7387-3516-0, 240 pp., 5³⁄₁₆ x 8 $14.99

To order, call 1-877-NEW-WRLD
Prices subject to change without notice
Order at Llewellyn.com 24 hours a day, 7 days a week

True Casefiles of a
PARANORMAL INVESTIGATOR

Stephen Lancaster

True Casefiles of a Paranormal Investigator
Stephen Lancaster

As a ghost hunter for nearly fifteen years, Stephen Lancaster's encounters with the paranormal range from the merely incredible to the downright terrifying. This gripping collection of true casefiles takes us behind the scenes of his most fascinating paranormal investigations. See what it's like to come face-to-face with an unearthly glowing woman in a dark cemetery, be attacked by invisible entities, talk to spirits using a flashlight, and dodge objects launched by a poltergeist. Every delicious detail is documented: the history and legends of each haunted location, what Stephen's thinking and feeling throughout each unimaginable encounter, and how he manages to capture ghost faces, spirit voices, a cowboy shadow man, otherworldly orbs, a music-loving spirit playing an antique piano, and other extraordinary paranormal evidence.

978-0-7387-3220-6, 240 pp., 5³⁄₁₆ x 8 $15.95

To order, call 1-877-NEW-WRLD
Prices subject to change without notice
Order at Llewellyn.com 24 hours a day, 7 days a week

MICHELLE BELANGER

"Michelle Belanger is without a doubt
the go-to person for paranormal
enthusiasts looking
to learn more."
—RYAN BUELL, FOUNDER OF THE
PARANORMAL RESEARCH SOCIETY

THE GHOST HUNTER'S SURVIVAL GUIDE

PROTECTION TECHNIQUES FOR
ENCOUNTERS WITH THE PARANORMAL

The Ghost Hunter's Survival Guide
*Protection Techniques for
Encounters With The Paranormal*
MICHELLE BELANGER

Ghosts can't hurt us, right? Guess again!

Chasing the unseen has become a popular American pastime, but how can we protect ourselves from mischievous ghosts, astral parasites, and malevolent spirits? Michelle Belanger, a rising star in the paranormal community, comes to the rescue with a self-defense program for ghost hunters—or anyone vulnerable to a spirit attack. Proven successful by Belanger and other paranormal investigators, these easy-to-learn mental exercises can be used to protect homes, shield against harmful entities, and remove unwanted spirit guests.

Interlacing each chapter is a gripping, true ghost investigation conducted by Belanger, which provides context for understanding when to use these potent defense strategies.

978-0-7387-1870-5, 288 pp., 6 x 9 $16.95

To order, call 1-877-NEW-WRLD
Prices subject to change without notice
Order at Llewellyn.com 24 hours a day, 7 days a week